ETpedia™

Business English

500 ideas for Business English teachers

G R
N J
S M P
H
A Z B
F O
Q X T

John Hughes and Robert McLarty

Series editor: John Hughes

www.myetpedia.com

ENGLISH TEACHING *professional*

ETpedia

500 ideas for Business English teachers

© John Hughes and Robert McLarty

The authors have asserted their rights in accordance with the Copyright, Designs and Patents Act (1988) to be identified as the authors of this work.

Published by:
Pavilion Publishing and Media Ltd
Rayford House
School Road
Hove BN3 5HX
UK
Tel: 01273 434 943
Fax: 01273 227 308

First published 2016

Photocopying permission

ISBN: 978-1-911028-20-8

PDF ebook ISBN: 978-1-911028-27-7

Epub ISBN: 978-1-911028-28-4

Kindle ISBN: 978-1-911028-29-1

Authors: John Hughes and Robert McLarty

Editor: Cathy Rogers

Production editor: Mike Benge, Pavilion Publishing and Media

Cover design: Emma Dawe, Pavilion Publishing and Media

Page layout and typesetting: Tony Pitt, Pavilion Publishing and Media

Printing: CMP Digital Print Solutions

Contents

Introduction

10 reasons for using this resource

1. Everything in one place

Business English teachers can find supplementary resources, teaching ideas, activities and tips in many different places. If you work at a language school, the shelves of your teachers' room might have many different publications, resource books and folders full of materials created by your colleagues. If you are teacher who travels to different companies to teach English, then perhaps you rely more on websites offering lesson plans and worksheets. The amount of materials for teachers these days can be overwhelming and also time-consuming to search through. The aim of this this resource book is to bring together a collection of ideas, tips, tools and techniques in one place for faster reference.

2. Clearly organised

This resource contains 50 units covering everything from preparing and planning your Business English course, activities for different business topics and a range of ideas for developing business communication skills. Each unit always has 10 points. Why 10? Well, if you're new to teaching Business English, reading our 10 tips on carrying out needs analysis will mean you can plan your course. Having 10 activities for practising the language of sales will help most teachers prepare a lesson on the topic. And knowing the 10 criteria that make an effective presentation will allow you to give detailed feedback.

3. New to Business English teaching

If you are teaching Business English for the first time ever, then this resource will provide you with all the basics to help you effectively plan a course and teach students who are in work or students who are planning future careers in business.

4. Experienced teachers

Perhaps you have been teaching Business English in companies or in universities or colleges for some time. Hopefully you'll find some ideas in this book that are familiar or which remind you of activities you haven't used for a while, and it'll also give you some fresh ideas to give your lessons a boost.

5. Supplementing your coursebook

If you are following a coursebook or a set of materials for a defined syllabus, then this resource can support that content with ways to lead into topics, expand the range of activity types, and suggest how to adapt the material to match learners' needs and interests.

6. Studying for a Business English qualification

Perhaps you are taking a formal qualification in teaching Business English such as the Certificate in International Business English Training (Cert IBET) or the LCCI First Certificate for Teachers of Business English. Or perhaps you are focusing on developing your business English skills as part of an MA qualification or the DELTA or Diploma in TESOL. For any teacher involved in this kind of ongoing professional development, this resource is an excellent reference with the lists of 10 acting as useful study tools.

7. Teacher trainers

If you are a teacher trainer or someone who needs to deliver staff training in the area of Business English, then use the checklists of ideas that this resource offers as a means to preparing your sessions.

8. Course planners and materials writers

Business English ETpedia includes information on needs analysis, planning and lists of business topics and skills with suggested exercise types. This means that course planners and writers will find it helpful in the development of course programmes.

9. Additional materials

As well as the resources offered in this resource, you will also find additional photocopiable worksheets in the Appendix. These worksheets relate to units in the resource and offer instant classroom activities.

10. More time

The one thing most teachers need is more time; more time to plan, more time to search for resources, more time to reflect on their teaching, and more time to develop their skills and knowledge for the Business English classroom. We hope that by offering you this collection of accessible ideas, you'll have more time to spend on developing your teaching in the way you would like.

"ETpedia saves hours of planning time and opens opportunities for variation, adaptation and even creating my own materials inspired by the ideas it offers."

Ayat Al-Tawel, teacher of Business English, Egypt

Introduction

10 ways to use this resource

This book has been written for different teachers at different stages of their Business English teaching career. It can be read and used in different ways according to your level of experience, need or interest.

1. Cover to cover

You could start at the beginning and read to the end. If you are finding out about teaching Business English for the first time, then the book will work as an introductory text to the subject.

2. Read a section

The contents page will direct you to different sections. In each section you will find units containing 10 ideas, tips, activities, questions or thoughts on a particular aspect of teaching. Some of the sections might not be immediately relevant to your context so you can leave these for later (when you might need them) and some sections will help you with immediate interests, concerns or questions.

3. Teacher's block

Just as writers sometimes have days when they can't write (a condition commonly referred to as 'writer's block'), there are days when teachers search desperately for ideas to help them come up with a lesson, but can't think of anything. We can call this 'teacher's block', and we hope this book will offer you some help with it. Open the book at any page and see if the 10 ideas on that page give you a new idea.

4. Teaching a new area of business

One reason that teachers enjoy Business English is that they are constantly coming into contact with students from different business backgrounds who need different types of English. This book suggests ways to learn about the new area of business and how to approach teaching the English needed.

5. Write in the book

Maybe you've tried one of the activities in the book or found an idea you liked. Make notes in the margin about why it worked or how you adapted it, so you can refer to it again later.

6. Helping colleagues

If you work with other teachers, then you've probably experienced a situation where a colleague is desperately searching for something to help improve their lesson. Perhaps you can help them out by suggesting they manage a lesson on meeting skills by using some of the ideas in Unit 31 on page 90. Or if they'd like to make more use of authentic materials, then show them the tips in Unit 47 on page 130.

7. Last-minute lessons

Most teachers have experienced the day when a colleague is off sick and they have been asked to teach a class at very short notice. You probably won't have much time to prepare, but you'll find enough ideas in Section 'Activities for business topics' (see page 39) to help you teach a complete and useful lesson.

8. More practice

Many students require extra practice on specific areas of English. For example, they might ask you for more speaking practice in your lesson (see Unit 24 on page 69) or perhaps you have noticed that a class needs more time to work on business writing (see Unit 41 on page 114).

9. Develop yourself

If you're at the stage of your teaching career where you feel you are ready for more of a challenge, you'll find some ideas in Unit 50 on page 137.

10. Write your own 10

Teaching is always evolving, developing and changing. More ideas can be added so why not visit the www.myetpedia.com. You can read blog posts from other teachers suggesting their own set of 10 ideas and you are invited to suggest your own 10 (see p173).

"I frequently use the ideas in ETpedia as a kind of checklist when preparing."

Mario Lecluyze, teacher trainer, Belgium

John Hughes ...

- ▶ taught his first Business English class in Poland in 1993. He then worked as a Business English teacher at language schools, in universities, and for companies including Gucci, Deloitte and Fiat.

- ▶ has managed Business English departments in Poland and Italy, carrying out language audits and needs analyses, course design and assessment.

- ▶ has trained many teachers from all over the world to work in the field of Business English, including training courses leading to the LCCI First Certificate in Teaching Business English qualification.

- ▶ has been the author or co-author on many Business English course books, including *Business Result, Successful Presentations, Successful Meetings* (Oxford University Press), *Success with BEC Vantage* (Summertown/Cengage Learning), and *Telephone English* (Macmillan).

- ▶ regularly gives talks and presentations on different English Language Teaching topics at international teacher's conferences and in online webinars. He also writes for journals including *English Teaching Professional* and *Modern English Teacher*.

Robert McLarty ...

- ▶ taught his first Business English class at International House, Hastings, in 1979. Since then he has worked as a Business English teacher in Paris and Oxford.

- ▶ has run Business English schools in Paris, Hastings and Oxford, designing courses, recruiting and training teachers and developing new products.

- ▶ has co-authored Business English books including *Business Basics, Quick Work* and *Business Focus* (Oxford University Press).

- ▶ has conceptualised and published a wide range of Business English coursebooks including *Business Result, Skills for Business Studies, Business one:one, Successful Presentations* and *Successful Meetings* (Oxford University Press).

- ▶ regularly gives talks on Business English, writes materials and articles, edits *Modern English Teacher* and is Principal Tutor at the Oxford Teachers' Academy.

Thanks and acknowledgements

The authors would like to thank everyone involved in the development of *Business English ETpedia*. In particular Cathy Rogers and the team at Pavilion Publishing including Fiona Richmond, Lyra-Marie Burton and Mike Benge. We'd also like to thank all the Business English teachers and trainers who gave feedback on our ideas and who shared their own.

What is Business English?

This section begins by defining what Business English is and looking at its position in relation to English language teaching in general. Anyone new to teaching Business English will find this section a useful introduction, and more experienced teachers will find it helpful as a summary of the key areas that go to make up Business English.

The first few units explain what Business English is and why students choose to take this kind of course in contrast to a more general English course. Unit 4 also addresses some of the typical concerns that teachers have who are new to Business English. So if you are the kind of teacher who never imagined you'd be teaching 'business', then this unit should allay any fears you might have.

Units 5 to 7 focus much more on some of the typical contexts in which Business English is taught. For example, you might be teaching one-to-one or in small groups. Often these kinds of lessons take place on company premises and away from the typical language school setting. On the other hand, there is a growing demand for Business English to be taught at college or university level to young adult students. In this context, classes can be large and your students won't have much personal experience of the world of work or business to draw upon.

If you are totally new to teaching Business English, then it's probably worth reading the whole of this section from beginning to end in order to give yourself a thorough introduction. For teachers with more experience of Business English, then you'll want to dip in to those units which provide you with additional ideas and support.

10 aspects of Business English

Most people picking up this book will be familiar with the terms ELT (English Language Teaching), TEFL (Teaching English as a Foreign Language), and TESOL (Teaching English to Speakers of Other Languages). They all refer, in very broad terms, to the world of teaching English to people who need the language for a whole variety of reasons.

However, one of the main reasons why many adult students learn English is because they want to get a job, build their career, or extend their professional skills. So many language teachers often find that they are teaching a type of English that is linked directly to the world of work and business; what is often referred to as *Business English* or *English for work*. Interestingly, when you ask different teachers to give you a single definition of what Business English is, you'll find a wide variety of views and comments. Here is a selection of definitions based on 10 different viewpoints which, when read together, provide a very useful introduction.

1. English for your job or the workplace

In Business English you are teaching students who don't necessarily need a general course in which they try to move up a level; instead they want English that will help them to do their current job or their future job more effectively. Some of these students won't be involved in private business necessarily. They might work in the public sector or for a charity, for example. But the term 'Business English' is often used generally to refer to anyone trying to work effectively using English, whether that means by reading legal documents, writing commercial terms, handling phone-calls and emails or dealing with international clients.

2. Time-effective English

Many business people are very busy and don't want to spend time studying every area of English. Business English is often concerned with the English that students need now and how they can learn it in the most time-effective (and cost-effective) way.

3. Business topics

Some students will need key vocabulary to talk about specific areas of business. For example, someone working in Human Resources might need specific vocabulary to talk about what it is they do or to carry out aspects of their role such as recruitment. Similarly, if you are teaching pre-work students in a university setting, you might teach English within the context of different subjects ranging from marketing to logistics, to environmental ethics. You won't necessarily teach the actual subject, but you will sometimes use texts about these topics.

4. Communication skills

Unlike general English, Business English includes helping students to communicate in certain ways that are common to business. These communication skills include giving presentations, participating in meetings, socialising and networking and writing business correspondence. Many business people take special training in communication skills in their own language so your job might be to provide the English they'll need. However, sometimes Business English teachers also need to give help with aspects of communication such as effective body language and using visual aids.

5. Communicative competence

In Business English we are usually more interested in whether a student can communicate effectively to complete a task rather than how much grammar or vocabulary they know. For example, a student with a lower level of English can sometimes be a more engaging presenter or a more effective negotiator than a student with advanced English. In other words, they use the English they have to its greatest effect along with the other personal skills they possess.

6. Training more than teaching

Some Business English teachers prefer to call themselves 'trainers'. It might be that the term 'trainer' sounds more professional in the business world, but it also reflects the fact that in Business English we often focus on helping the students to be better at what they do with the English they already have. (Note that throughout this book we use 'teacher' and 'trainer' interchangeably.)

7. Businesslike as well as about business

Given that many of your students will be professional people working in company environments, the term Business English often implies a certain expectation that the teacher will be equally professional and businesslike. This influences every aspect of the job, from how you present yourself to the appearance and quality of the teaching materials you use.

8. Client and colleague English

Business English is also about the type of people that your students will need to communicate with. Typically, we think of business people talking to clients and customers who are interested in buying and selling. But in today's international world, your students will also need English to communicate with their colleagues and counterparts in other countries.

9. Specific and general English

Sometimes you'll meet a teacher working with business students and they'll say, 'We don't really do business English; my students want general English.' What they often mean is that their students aren't interested in reading and discussing texts about, for example, the stockmarket. Instead they want to talk about everyday topics. The point is that Business English can include being able to discuss general subjects when making conversation with colleagues and clients. After all, a large part of doing business is about relationship-building and social English.

10. English for travel

Many Business English students will take your course because they travel and use English in different parts of the world. They might need English to check in, to order food, or to take a taxi. It's all part of the content and approach that forms what we call Business English.

10 reasons why students choose Business English

There is a wide range of reasons for people studying Business English. Why they have chosen this course, or had it chosen for them quite often, will have a huge impact on how you plan and deliver the courses.

1. Aspirations

Many teenagers and young adult students soon realise that English is vital if they plan on having a career in skilled industries. In some countries, when students go to colleges to study technical courses, English lessons might be included as part of their programme.

2. International businesses

With so many businesses relying on international trade, employees often find that they have to be able to use some English as a medium of communication with colleagues and clients in a variety of countries. Note that these won't just be with people from countries where English is the first language, but also from countries where English is commonly used as a lingua franca.

3. Promotion

Anyone who is keen to get promoted will often need to develop more skills or to improve existing skills. Being able to communicate effectively in English is often one of those skills and may be necessary for anyone trying move up the career ladder.

4. Changing jobs

As with getting promoted, some of your students might be on your course with the aim of gaining a level of English that will help them apply for jobs with other companies.

5. A reward for good performance

Some companies offer the incentive of training as a reward for good work or even for loyalty.

6. A specific job to do

One of the best teaching situations is when the participant needs training to fulfil a specific role. The needs will be clear, motivation will be high and all stakeholders will be pushing for a successful outcome.

7. Documentation in English

As globalisation continues, more and more employees find themselves surrounded by reporting and administrative systems in English. The spread of IT has been a real driver of growth for the English language and a lot of back-office employees are finding themselves having to deal with data in English. They might not ever need to speak English, but they still need to improve their reading, writing and vocabulary.

8. The company language

We often think that English is used only in business for external communications with people overseas, but for many companies English is also the internal company language. For example, a company in Italy could be taken over by a multinational with branches and divisions all over the world – in this situation, the new 'parent' company might insist that all internal communication, especially documentation, is now carried out in English.

9. University studies

Students at university often study subjects such as business or finance which require a good level of English. This might be because lectures are given in English and the fact that so much of the academic literature for these kinds of course will also be in English.

10. Lots of other reasons or none at all

You will also find that a large number of students simply take the course because it is there. The company offers it and staff members accept it without necessarily having a real and tangible need. A careful balance of English for work, travel and socialising is often necessary in these cases.

"Choosing Business English (instead of general English) ensures the language focus is relevant and that the topics and tasks prepare professional people for the specific situations they will encounter in their working lives, while making the most of their limited time."

Hannah Murphy, Principal, OIE Oxford, UK

Unit 2

10 things that can make Business English different from general English

Although around 90% of the words you will be teaching are the same in both general and Business English courses, there are some major differences which you will need to bear in mind. They will affect the way you manage the course and the way your teaching is perceived by the participants. Here are 10 ways in which Business English courses are often different from general courses.

1. Course length

Courses for companies and professional individuals tend to be shorter in Business English. They have to fit in around busy work schedules and sometimes students may only be with you for a few months. For this reason, your aims and objectives will often be based on the immediate or short-term needs.

2. Needs analysis and course planning

You may have a coursebook or programme to follow, but it's always important to find out the needs of your students and reflect those needs in your planning (see Unit 9 on p26). Let your students play a key role in the planning and content of the course.

3. Defining the students

In general English we often define students in terms of level and then put them into classes accordingly. When teaching in businesses, level is important but we also define students in other ways. For example, are they already in work and therefore have lots of experience? Or are they pre-work, so that you might have to teach them about business concepts as well? We can also define and group them according to their job profile; so even though a group of engineers may have different general English levels, it might make sense to put them in the same class in order to work with their specialist area of English.

4. Tangible results

On a Business English course the students are often sponsored by their company. Like any investment, the company expects a quantifiable return which means that the students have to be noticeably better at a work-related aspect of English after the course. Ideally, students should leave the class feeling that what they have just learnt can be instantly used in their workplace. The company itself may also expect to see clearly-defined results being achieved in a cost-effective way.

5. Working with experts

A lot of the expertise in a lesson comes from your students. In other words, they know what their job is about and will probably need to teach you about it. Your job is to provide them with the English to be able to talk about it and carry it out.

6. The role of the teacher

In Business English, the words used to describe the role of the teacher often differ from those used to describe teaching in a school situation with general English courses. Sometimes you might be referred to as a 'trainer', a 'coach', a 'language consultant' or even as a 'service provider' delivering English to your client-student. These roles reflect the styles and approaches to teaching English that can emerge in the Business English context.

7. Location

Typically, English teachers are used to working in a classroom in a school, but teaching in the Business English context often requires a different setting. You might have access to a well-equipped training room or sometimes you might have to work with the student at his or her desk. You could find yourself teaching students on a factory floor or perhaps delivering a one-to-one lesson over the phone or via skype. Flexibility is a key skill for any Business English teacher.

8. The stakeholders

Unlike in a general English class where there is usually one main stakeholder – the student – or perhaps also the parents of a younger student, in business the other stakeholders in the course might include people such as the head of training, the student's boss, or even the owner or managing director of the company. So the teacher will often need to balance the needs and interests of a number of different stakeholders.

9. Teacher professionalism

Of course teachers should have a professional attitude to their job in any situation, but in a business context you may need to follow certain dress codes or adhere to strict rules when on the company premises. In other words you need to aim to fit into the business culture of the company you are working with.

10. Developing yourself

One key reason why many teachers prefer Business English to general English is that you start to learn so much about different areas of business. Many of your students are such experts in their field (see 5) that they share their knowledge with you. So in return for teaching them English, you can learn about a whole range of topics.

"I prefer teaching Business English to general English as I can help my learners focus on developing their careers and improving workplace performance. An improvement in their general English ability is a natural by-product."

Mike Hogan, Director of Teacher Training, York Associates, UK

Unit 3

10 concerns about teaching Business English

Teachers who start out teaching general English are often worried about switching to Business English. It should be no more worrying than taking on any new type of course, such as an exam preparation course or a complete beginners' class. Many people assume because they have little experience of the business world that this will in some way be found out. In fact, teaching Business English is an extraordinary opportunity to learn about a whole range of different professions simply by being an interested and active listener. You may recognise some of the thoughts in this list.

1. **'I don't know anything about business.'**

   Above all you are a teacher of English and it is the language in which you are an expert. Your classes and individual students come to you to improve their performance in English and expect your help. They will not expect you to be an expert in all the different professional areas they come from. They are also very keen to discuss things other than their work occasionally.

2. **'How can I teach concepts and vocabulary I don't understand?'**

   Your main objective is to teach English and as you gain experience in different work-related courses you will start to understand more and more about business, certainly enough to start asking questions which will activate language from your students. If you come across a term or a concept you don't understand, it is perfectly natural and useful to ask the class to try and explain it in English.

3. **'My class know much more than I do.'**

   This is undoubtedly true about many things, but not English and how to teach it. Use what the class know to teach them what they do not know. In other words, take advantage of their professional knowledge to improve their English by using role plays, presentations and case-studies which require them to transfer their knowledge into English.

4. **'They are all older than me.'**

   This is a regular comment among newer teachers, but be assured that at a certain time it will no longer be true! In the meantime make sure you act in a mature, professional way and no-one will judge you on your age as long as you do your job well.

5. **'They don't always do the homework and sometimes don't attend class.'**

   Inevitably working people are going to be too busy to attend their language classes if they have other priorities at work. Always let them know what they have missed and give them access to any worksheets you have handed out or online links you would like to them to study. With a class which has regular absentees, make sure that your lessons are self-contained and do not rely on attendance over a period of time. Try and plan homework which can be done quickly and anywhere, e.g. a short exercise, an email or a quick listening exercise.

6. **'Will I have to dress very smartly?'**

   You will have to dress in a professional, neat way because you are representing your school often on the client's premises. It also helps to convey a sense of 'I know what I am doing'.

7. 'I like teaching general English and there isn't much in Business English.'

In fact there is a lot of what you might call 'general English' in Business English. Your students still need to learn grammar, vocabulary, pronunciation and the four skills (reading, writing, speaking and listening). So all the skills you have developed in teaching English elsewhere, including to young learners and teenagers, still apply.

8. 'I like being in charge and sticking to the plan.'

In Business English classes you always have to be prepared to abandon the plan and go with a topic the group needs to work on. This typically happens when there is a professional need to look at a particular topic, a visitor is coming or someone has a presentation to prepare, or the industry is in the news and the class want to discuss it in English. Your role at this point is to facilitate and monitor the language used. Keep the planned lesson for another day.

9. 'The course is very short.'

Some Business English classes can be as short as 10 to 15 hours. It is important that you maximise the teaching time to really make a difference. Choose one or two clear objectives and work on them. Improving speaking or writing skills can easily be addressed in a short course with noticeable improvements if the lessons are carefully tailored to the participants' needs. It might be that you have to leave out some of your favourite lesson types such as grammar or reading because they are not really time-effective.

10. 'Business English is boring.'

This is the most incorrect assumption or concern of all. Business is fascinating because it isn't just about how to buy or sell, or make money. Every business and every organisation is different, so it's rare to find any student who doesn't have an interesting job. The trick is to find out what is relevant to the student, and then work on relevant scenarios and language. Asking question after question allows you to build up your understanding of the job while stretching your students' ability to discuss it in English.

"Before my first Business English class, I feared that the level of intellect of my students would be way beyond me and any discussions would go right over my head. It turned out they were normal people who enjoyed a good laugh or game to balance out the serious stuff just as much as any other class."

Angie Conti, Academic Manager, Malta

Unit 4

10 typical Business English teaching contexts

When a teacher tells you they teach Business English classes you might imagine something very different to the context they actually teach in. Depending on the country, the client and the premises, any number of the following might be the 'training' room. Wherever you are doing the teaching it will be up to you to take advantage of the circumstances to make the lessons as effective as possible.

1. In a meeting room

Some Business English classes take place on the company premises, often in a meeting room around a large table. This makes students feel at home, but makes it less easy for the teacher to rearrange furniture to suit activities. On the other hand, such rooms often have good technology such as internal phones, internet connections and data projectors which can be used to great effect.

2. In the student's own office

This is especially true for one-to-one lessons. Note that the dynamics of the student sitting on one side of a big desk and you on the other can sometimes make the lesson too formal, so try to sit together at a table in the office. On a positive note, working in the student's office can give you a real insight into their working lives and help you plan and teach accordingly.

3. On the factory floor

If you are teaching students whose job is in a factory, then you might need to run your lessons literally 'on the job'. This might mean you are putting up with external noise or interruptions but you can turn this kind of situation to your advantage by making the lessons very hands-on. For example, students can explain how the factory works and you can start to introduce the language they need to make their explanations more effective.

4. On the telephone

Given that speaking in English over the phone is something that challenges many students, teaching over the phone is a great opportunity to develop the students' confidence and ability to speak and listen in English. Note that you can also use teleconference equipment to teach groups of students.

5. Via skype or facetime

Online video conference technology such as Skype or Facetime provides a useful medium for one-to-one and small group teaching, allowing 24/7 teaching in a very flexible way. The lessons can be recorded and reviewed by those present as well as those who were unable to attend.

6. At home

Intensive courses for a weekend, a week or more with the teacher acting both as host and teacher are increasingly common and accredited in the UK by the British Council. The advantage to the learner is that they are in a relaxed, totally immersed environment learning in both formal lessons and informal social settings.

7. At a language school with mixed nationalities

Multilingual classes in English-speaking countries offer a wide range of Business English classes with the added benefit that there is a genuine need to communicate in the target language and a genuine information gap as students swap ideas and share experiences.

8. In a company training room

Some large companies with a real interest in lifelong learning have great facilities for training. Business English courses in this context often take place in purpose-built rooms with great equipment.

9. At university

As more and more students in higher education realise that they will probably need English to get a decent job, universities are offering Business English. These courses often cover not only the language of business but some of the concepts as well.

10. In fact, anywhere!

Teaching Business English and English for work can take place virtually anywhere. The two authors of this book have also taught English to people who needed it for their job inside a helicopter, in a home appliances showroom, at a conference centre, on a train to Warsaw, in a travel agent, underneath the chassis of a car, on a building site, in a chauffeured car, in the nightwear department of a Paris store, in a restaurant, and many more places.

Unit 4

> "I taught a Finn on the beach once. He needed English for video conferencing and made his colleagues jealous by calling from the beach."
>
> **Sue Annan, Training and Business English Co-ordinator, St Brelade's College, Jersey**

10 tips for teaching one-to-one and small groups

Business English lessons are often with one student or small groups. However, many teacher-training courses do not deal with the dynamics of small group or individual teaching even though most teachers will probably have an opportunity to teach them quite early in their career. There are some real advantages to working with small groups as you can use activities which simply would not work in a large class.

1. Use their expertise

The smaller the group, the easier it is to fit the programme to the learners' needs. The lexical and functional areas your students would like you to cover might be very specialised. Use your students' knowledge, their documents and their scenarios to inform the course content. For the learner, whether they are a chemist, a pilot or a legal assistant, the language will automatically be more memorable and easier to retain because they have felt a genuine need to use it.

2. Be proactive right from the start

In a large group, it is understandable that a number of students are less talkative and appear less interested than others. In a small group, however, each student has a real opportunity not only to contribute actively, but also to influence the shape of the lessons and the direction of the course. From the start, encourage students to ask questions and offer opinions, not only about the subject of the lesson but also about other areas they would like to explore.

3. Conversations have to be two-way

One of the easiest traps to fall into is the one way conversation where everything is initiated by the teacher. Practise turn-taking by setting up five minute sessions where only the class can initiate the conversation and have them score points for interest and change of subject rather than just grammatical accuracy. The more your learners can transfer their normal adult L1 conversation skills into English, the better they will communicate.

4. Vary your correction technique

You will come across a wide array of Business English learners with very different attitudes to correction. Some will expect constant correction, others want the correction but appear to ignore it and continue to make the same mistakes, while others like errors noted down so as not to interrupt the communicative flow. Peer correction should be developed, but do be aware of the hierarchical issues in your class, particularly if they are all from the same company. Some learners are loathe to be corrected by anyone other than the teacher.

5. Seating arrangements

For small groups and one-to-one classes, seating arrangements can be very important. For groups, make sure you take into account the personalities and any hierarchy issues. Ensure the layout allows for communication, but also permits you to stand up and present if necessary. In one-to-one classes you may prefer to work from sheets of A2 or A3 or with a tablet or laptop rather than standing up at a whiteboard.

6. Record regularly

Easy access to recording technology (such as voice recording on a phone) makes it a realistic and useful tool for smaller groups. Get students into the habit of recording themselves and listening to their voice. The technique allows them to see the importance of pronunciation and to highlight where they can realistically improve. Recordings also act as a great point of comparison at the start and end of a course and are a very useful homework activity for those who are too busy to do more traditional exercises.

7. Changing the pace

Teaching one-to-one and small groups for long classes can be highly intensive. It's possible that your student or students have requested personal classes in order to get the maximum amount of time speaking and listening to you. However, you will still need to vary the pace of the lesson and to take breaks from just talking. Include moments where the pace and style of the lesson changes. Don't be afraid to have students do a quick exercise on their own or show a short video clip to break up the lesson. Your students will also probably welcome the opportunity for a short break from talking.

8. Experiment with your teaching approach

With older classes, your learners might not have been language students for quite a while. This means that the way they react to pedagogic materials might not necessarily be in quite the way you expect. Some students could find role playing difficult, others won't enjoy controlled practice, and perhaps a few students won't like a discovery approach for learning language – they'll want you to tell them the grammar rule, for example. Be prepared to experiment with what works and what doesn't.

9. Change the location

To inject variety into a lesson with one student or a small group, suggest having a lesson somewhere else. Take them out of the usual classroom and go for a walk round the building or agree to meet at a café, perhaps, or – for lessons that normally take place on company premises – suggest your students come to your normal language school for the day. A change of environment can really stimulate learning.

10. Give responsibility

Introduce the idea of role reversal by asking a learner to teach the rest of the class (or you). Being able to illustrate, explain, describe or demonstrate a skill or a topic in English is a highly motivating activity which takes the focus away from the teacher and creates genuine learner-centredness. Giving all students the chance to do this at least once in the course will prove very popular and effective.

10 differences between in-work and pre-work Business English

We can categorise Business English students in two general ways. In-work students (sometimes referred to as in-service) are already working. Pre-work (or pre-service) are those that are still studying. This essential difference can affect your lessons in the following ways.

1. Experience

The in-work (IW) learner has a career and a complete understanding of their position. They understand, therefore, precisely what they need or potentially will need to do in English. The pre-work (PW) learner lacks this experience and brings less professional knowledge to the course. Both require Business English, but the content of the course will be quite different.

2. The theory behind the job

The IW learner is unlikely to need to learn business theory whereas the PW student will still have gaps in this part of their knowledge. Business theories (e.g. approaches to management, types of company structure) are a good context for learning vocabulary for the PW learner while the IW learners will be keener to acquire the language needed to communicate in very practical situations such as writing emails, attending meetings or chatting to colleagues all in English.

3. Learning experience

Many IW learners may not have been in a formal learning situation for a while and will lack the study skills of the PW learner who will be used to taking notes, doing research, managing projects with fellow students and submitting written work. Traditional forms of homework might not always be that appealing to the IW learner so it is best to ask them to do homework tasks which fit into their normal professional practices such as writing an email or preparing some PowerPoint slides.

4. Flexibility

With a PW course, students will be expected to attend lessons at certain times and reports may be produced to indicate attendance. This also might be true for the IW course, but the reality is that IW students will tend to be absent and late more often because of outside work pressures. As a result, you might need to build in lots more in-class recycling and revision activities for the IW learners who cannot attend on a regular or punctual basis.

5. Curriculum

IW learners will have a much clearer idea of the situational language and vocabulary as well as the specific skills they need to work on. If they do not have to negotiate in their first language, then it is unlikely they will need to learn to do it in English. The same will be the case for all the communication skills, email, telephone, meetings etc. As a result, planning a targeted curriculum is much easier for IW learners. For PW students, the curriculum is normally defined for them before the course because the way they will actually be using English is still an unknown.

6. Tests and exams

Quite often PW learners are in an environment where they will have to take a test or exam at the end of the academic year, so you will need to teach towards that. For IW learners you will probably use testing less because the real test is whether than can carry out their current job in English. Nevertheless, some companies may expect their employees to be tested regularly and results may need to be given to a manager. If this is the case, then clarify the format of these tests early and prepare students for them.

7. Short term and long term view

Because a PW course is often delivered in a higher education institution, your students are usually studying full-time so there is time for homework, revision, project work and so on. There is also time to take a longer view and build up their general English level at the same time, so there is room for grammar and everyday vocabulary and expressions. With IW classes, where the course length can be much shorter, the main aim will be to improve their ability to work in English; this means that in theory every lesson needs a 'takeaway' – something that they can use in their job after the lesson.

8. Motivation

IW learners who have asked for the course in order to perform better professionally have a strong intrinsic motivation to succeed. They might also have been put forward by their manager, giving them a sound extrinsic motivation as well. On the other hand, some IW learners are on the course just because it is on offer, in which case their motivation might not be as clear. PW classes, as on a general English course, will be made up of students who are highly motivated and those who are less motivated and less keen to contribute.

9. Attitude to the teacher

With PW learners you will often be asked to teach both business concepts and the language of business. There is a lot of knowledge to transfer and you – as the teacher – are in charge of that transfer. You will also probably be involved in the testing and the assessment at the end of the session. Your role is clearly defined and the majority of students will understand it and behave normally just like in most of their classes. With IW learners the role is less traditional; you are there to help them work more effectively. Quite how you do this will depend on the make-up of the group, their attitude towards English, the relationship you build with them and the usefulness of the lessons you give. Don't worry if you sometimes come across resentment towards learning English. This is understandable among learners of a certain age who never expected they'd have to try and learn a new language at their stage in life.

10. Out of class pressures

With IW learners we sometimes forget that they are trying to learn English on top of everything else in their already busy lives. Not only do the participants have to come before or after work, or sometimes instead of lunch, they then have to go back to their job and families and fit in homework, revision and any other preparation the course requires. On the other hand, PW learners might be studying other subjects at their school or college so bear in mind the rest of their workload.

10 characteristics of teaching in-company

One of the main differences about teaching Business English is that you will often be asked to teach in-work students on the company's premises. For new teachers this can be a little strange at first and requires a bit more planning than just going to school to teach your classes. Here are 10 points to bear in mind.

1. The logistics

Travelling to a company means planning how you are going to get there and how much time you'll need. You'll need the phone number of a contact person at the company in case you are delayed by traffic or you need to call in sick. And once you are at the company, subsequent lessons might take place in different locations so check you have enough time to get from one lesson to another.

2. Rules and regulations

One of the first things to understand as a Business English teacher is that when you are on the company premises you have to follow their rules and regulations. Identity cards, security checks and health and safety issues might become a regular part of your working day.

3. No colleagues

Unlike working in a language school or some other institution, you are quite likely to be the only English teacher on site. This means you have no one to get ideas from, no staffroom to relax in between lessons and no colleagues to interact with. A number of teachers find this quite difficult at first.

4. The face of the school

Because you are probably the only teacher on site, you are also automatically the face of the school. This means that as well as teaching you have to develop your client relation skills and look the part. Employees who don't follow the courses will know who you are and if your course goes well there is always the chance of an increase in business the following term.

5. Local knowledge

The longer you work in a company, the more you will understand how it works, what times of the year are busy, who the main customers are, how competitive the market is and so on. This insider knowledge will help you to develop more meaningful and useful lessons. Actively find out as much as you can about the company; don't be afraid to ask questions. Become an expert in what the company does.

6. Authentic location

Teaching in-company allows you to teach them the English they need in the place they need it. The authenticity of the situation is important and you can access samples, documents and sales literature, which will all be of use to you.

7. Luggage

One of the drawbacks of being on site is that you often have to carry everything with you. You might be in the same teaching room each time you go there, but there might not be a place to store things. Having to take all the materials for the day along with any equipment will always require some planning.

8. Shared background

With in-company teaching one of the advantages is that all the learners share the same background. This means there are common themes and topics which can be addressed, specific vocabulary areas which everyone needs and company events which can be included in the teaching programme. One of the benefits of an in-company teaching programme is that it helps different departments learn about each other through the medium of English.

9. Cover

It is highly unlikely you will be replaced if you are sick for a day on an in-company course. What usually happens is that the class is cancelled and you will have to try and make up the lesson at a later date.

10. Part of the furniture

When you have been teaching at a particular company for a number of years you might well become a sort of unofficial English adviser. Your old and new students will know you and that you are a safe pair of hands to turn to for tasks like checking a translation or informally helping someone with their presentation preparation.

"Giving lessons in a company (instead of in a school) provides a constant source of new teaching ideas because you experience at first hand students' everyday working reality."

David Grant, author and trainer, Nantes, France

Preparation and planning

One feature of Business English that distinguishes it from many other course types is that a great deal of emphasis is put on the use of a needs analysis stage to find out what students want and need from their course. The first units in this section deal with what a needs analysis is and why you might use one, especially on courses with students who already use English in their job.

This section also gives you tips on how to broaden your search for information about the students' language needs so that you get the full picture. From this research you will want to start planning a course. Sometimes you'll find a published course book which serves your needs, and on other courses you will want to tailor the materials and course aims to specific needs. So there's a unit giving advice on how to plan your course accordingly.

10 tips on carrying out a needs analysis

Carrying out a language needs analysis is a key difference between Business English and following a fixed curriculum on a general English course. The aim is to find out what your students need to gain from the course and then design the course towards those needs. So if you are working with a student who needs English to give presentations on the subject of data management, then you should try to help them become effective at doing this. Of course, teaching to the student's needs is relatively straight-forward in a one-to-one class. But when you have a group of students with different needs, you have to find ways to balance any difference in interests.

1. The student's level

When you first meet a student you need to establish his or her level of English. This could be done using a placement test, but you also want to meet the student face-to-face if possible. That's because a Business English student might score low (or possibly high) on a placement test which measures their general English level, but when it comes to performing their job in English, the student might be more or less effective than their general level suggests.

2. What? Who? How?

Many needs analysis questionnaires often include a list of extensive questions and tick boxes. Students can either fill these in on their own or you can use them as the basis of an interview. It's useful to remember that at the core of any needs analysis are three key questions:

▶ What do you communicate about in your work? (the business specialisms and topics)

▶ Who do you communicate with? (colleagues, clients, nationalities, job titles)

▶ How do you communicate? (by phone, via Skype, face-to-face in meetings, by email)

Any other questions that are asked in a needs analysis will probably relate to these three central questions.

3. Too much information

While it's important to find out lots about the student or students, there's a danger that we ask our students for too much information. The result is that we have so many needs and directions to follow that we don't know where to start. Also, our student's expectations might be set too high, believing that you will be able to address all the needs in an unrealistic length of time. So at the first meeting, if your students has lots of requests, try to prioritise them. If they need to give an important presentation in three weeks' time, then that's a good starting point. If they request report writing because they think they might have to do this sometime in the future, it can be dealt with later.

4. Balancing the needs of a group

You might have a group of students who all need the same kind of English; perhaps they all work in the same department or in the same field of business. If so, you can probably balance their needs and requirements. But many more classes include students from different departments or companies who all want to improve their English, but also have individual needs. In this case, it's important to make everyone's needs 'public' so every student is aware of the needs of their colleagues. Sometimes you might even want to say in class that a certain language area will be more useful for some students than others.

5. Pie-chart completion

A good way of collating needs in a group and to show the group how varied the needs are is to ask them to complete a simple pie-chart. They all draw a large circle and slice it up into the different areas they want to cover on the course. You can give them a choice comprising Grammar, Vocabulary, Pronunciation, Meetings, Telephoning, Writing, Socialising, Presentations and Specific language. The percentages they choose for the different areas will be reflected in their pie-charts. You can then collate these wishes into a group pie-chart reflecting the contents of the course as asked for by the participants.

6. First lesson presentations

To get a snapshot of the level and needs of the group you can ask them to do a short presentation at the first lesson. Ask them to talk about their job, who they work with, what they do in English and what they would like to achieve on the course. Give them time to think about what they are going to say. You could also put them in pairs and have them present to each other before asking them to present to the whole class. It's a useful way for the students to get to know each other and it provides you with plenty of information for course planning as well as finding out what areas of English will need the most work.

7. Ongoing needs analysis

No matter how careful and thorough your needs analysis is, there will be areas to work on which nobody will have mentioned or noticed. As the course develops, always be aware that needs might change or new ones emerge. Take time during a course to ask students if their needs are being met; this could take the form of an informal conversation at the end of a lesson or you could ask them to complete a short feedback form.

8. Feedback

We often mention feedback in this book because it is such a key element to good Business English teaching. A simple question after a lesson is to ask what happened during it – 'What did we do today?' The class needs to be aware not only of what happened, but also why it happened, in other words to understand the approach and pedagogy as well as simply describing the content. They need to evaluate the usefulness of activities and of their own contribution. They need to learn what they need you for, but also how much they need to help themselves.

9. Email Q and A

Before and during the course, a regular flow of information can happen via email or a class Facebook page. This allows you to communicate with the class and them with you. This is of use at the needs analysis stage but also as the course is rolled out. Questions can be asked and answers given or suggestions made by all participants.

10. Ways and means

One other useful way of adding value to the needs analysis is to ask participants to consider not only what they want to achieve, but how they are going to do it. If they want to increase their active vocabulary they will need to add something like 'by learning 20 new words a week'. If they want to increase their confidence in English on the telephone they can add 'by initiating at least one call a week in English'. These individual contracts will help them stay motivated and ultimately improve more quickly.

10 sets of questions to find out about a student's needs

Whether you plan to have students fill in a questionnaire at the beginning of course or you are going to interview them, it's useful to draw from a bank of questions. The 10 sets of questions below are designed to help you do this. Not all of them will always be relevant in every situation but they should form the basis for a fairly complete needs analysis.

1. Personal details

What's your name?

Where are you from?

2. Your job

What do you do?

What does that mean?

What is a typical day?

How did you get to this position? Were your studies useful?

What is the best/worst thing about your job?

When you meet someone socially, what do you say your job is?

3. Your company

Who do you work for?

What is your main product/service/activity?

When was the company founded and why?

Has your company got a website in English?

Which countries does the company work with/buy from/sell to/partner with?

4. People in your work

Who do communicate with in English on a day-to-day basis?

Do you mainly communicate with clients or colleagues?

What nationalities do you speak or write to in English?

What do you communicate about?

5. English in your job

How often do you use English in your job?

When do you use it most?

What do you find difficult to do in English?

6. Areas of work

How much do you already use English words to talk about your area of work?

What aspects of your work do you want to be able to talk about in English?

Would you describe the English you need as 'specialist English' or 'general English'? Why?

7. Communication skills

Which do you think is more important for you: speaking in English or writing in English?
How often do you use English in the following situations?

- ▶ Social situations with small talk.
- ▶ On the phone.
- ▶ To give or listen to presentations.
- ▶ To attend and participate in meetings and discussion.
- ▶ To solve problems in teams.
- ▶ To negotiate.
- ▶ Travelling for work.

What are some other typical situations when you use English?

8. Previous learning

Have you studied English before?
What courses/exams have you taken?
What did you enjoy about the course?
Do you have any ways you like to learn? (e.g. conversation, online, writing things down.)

9. The course

Who wants you to take this course? You? Your boss? Someone else?
Why do you/they want you to take it?
How much time can you spend on studying English outside of class?

10. Priorities

Can you rank these in order of importance?
(1 = most important for my job, 7 = least important for my job)
Afterwards give reasons for your answers.

Speaking

Listening

Reading

Writing

Grammar

Vocabulary

Pronunciation

▶▶ See photocopiable needs analysis form on p145.

ETpedia: 500 ideas for Business English teachers © Pavilion Publishing and Media Ltd and its licensors 2016.

Unit 10

10 sources of information in the planning process

It is important to remember that you are not alone when planning your courses and there are a number of people and other sources of information you can consult during the planning stage. You want to arrive at a stage where you have a reasonable knowledge of the company and the industry it is in, as well as a good understanding of the jobs the participants do in the company and any current issues.

1. Training manager

The person who organised the course will be the best point of contact for you. They will know the participants on a personal level, will understand the attitude of the company towards training and will be happy to answer your questions. As the course progresses keep them informed of progress and any issues which arise, such as absenteeism, etc.

2. Academic co-ordinator or manager

You will have been allocated to this course by someone at your language school, unless you are self-employed, and they will be able to provide you with entry test results, agreed objectives, lengths of courses, any materials to be provided and the rationale behind the groupings.

3. Previous or current teachers

People who have already taught in the company will be able to fill you in on the type of lessons which have been successful, the attitude of participants to homework, any cultural information which might be of use and any useful 'housekeeping' information, e.g. how to get there, where you can get photocopies made, where the vending machines and toilets are, etc.

4. The student's line manager

In many cases a student's boss may have suggested that the employee needs English lessons. It can be helpful to talk to this person to find out their reasons why and to know what their expectations are.

5. The class

From your first contact with them, the class will be an excellent source of information. Encourage them to let you have authentic documents about the company and the kind of documents they use or have to produce in English. Let them show you where they work so you get a clearer understanding of their working context and get regular feedback on your teaching to make sure you are giving them what they need.

6. Website

All companies and professional associations have a strong online presence these days and they can provide you with a great range of useful texts, images, graphs and charts. Mission statements, annual reports, product factsheets and location data will all help provide useful material to build lessons around. It sounds obvious, but a company history about their own employer will always be more intrinsically interesting than that of another firm.

7. YouTube

A company's online presence often extends to YouTube where clips about the company, its products, its processes or its people can often be found. If you cannot find anything specific to the company, there will probably be clips linked to the industrial area they operate in. Video clips are an excellent way of getting into specialised vocabulary as participants explain processes and procedures, name vocabulary items or write commentaries and voice overs to them.

8. News

A Google search will retrieve a large number of references to the company where it has been mentioned in the press. Again, if the company is small you might need to find articles about the industry rather than the specific firm. Texts found can be used to contextualise grammar or vocabulary as a starting point for discussion or the basis for skills-based activities. Short texts or individual sentences can be used as dictation-based warmers for practising listening and spelling.

9. Advertising

Companies advertise in many different ways depending on their size and their marketing strategy. If their business model is B2B (where their customers are other companies) rather than B2C (where they are selling to the general public) then their communication channels will be different. On a very general level, their logo, corporate colours, slogan, mission statement are all starting points to discuss their strategy and values. Advertisements in trade journals, brochures, promotional accessories and commercial presentations are also a rich source of further information about them.

10. Customers and suppliers

Any information you can find out about their partners is also useful for you in planning courses. What nationality are the key customers? Do they have many? Where are the suppliers based? What are the regular communication channels for dealing with them? What language is used in dealing with them? These questions will all feed into the needs analysis you have done and will keep the course engaging and relevant.

"Business English is all about helping learners to successfully perform in communicative events in English. In order to facilitate this we need to start by identifying what communicative events learners need to perform in, with whom and in which context(s), in other words, conduct a needs analysis."

Claire Hart, Business English trainer and author, Germany

Unit 11

10 typical departments in a company

One of the things you will need to know is what the main departments of a company do and how they relate to each other. This will help you understand more easily the kind of professional situations your students are likely to find themselves in and what they will need to do in English. Obviously, the larger the company, the more people they will have in each department. In smaller firms one or two people could make up the entire department.

1. Finance

Depending on the size of the company there will be people responsible for the following: treasury (cash-flow), accounts payable (settling invoices), management accounts, tax and financial analysis. There are aspects of the department which are for purely internal purposes, analysing profit margins or preparing monthly sales figures, and others which are more do with external regulations such as preparing accounts for external audit or compliance.

2. Human Resources

HR is responsible for recruitment, training, appraisal, salary and conditions, payroll, pensions, professional development and grievance procedures. They are usually responsible for setting up the type of course you might be running.

3. Research

Depending on the industrial sector, research (or research & development) is responsible for initial studies on finding and testing new products. They are also responsible for improving products, making them more durable, easier to produce, more efficient and so on. Quality departments check finished goods are up to standard and are permanently analysing processes to improve the standards.

4. Production

This operational department is responsible for managing the output from the company's plants or manufacturing facilities. Depending on the industry, they could be using raw materials to produce a chemical product like paint or assembling sets of parts to produce an electronic device, for example. Production will work closely with logistics to move the finished products on.

5. Logistics

Ensuring that the parts and raw materials get to the plant on time and the finished goods get to the wholesaler or direct to the customer is the responsibility of the logistics or distribution department. Requiring careful planning and attention to detail, this department is responsible for transportation and stocking.

6. Sales

Sales departments operate in different ways according to the industry, but in general they are responsible for finding and keeping customers. Some customers will be so important they will be part of a key account strategy, while others become customers when they need a particular product or service. The follow-up to these customers is known as after-sales service and can involve support and advice to the new customer. Sales staff require a very clear understanding of their services and how they can fit a customer's needs.

7. Marketing

Often working in tandem with sales, marketing is responsible for finding out what customers need, getting the new product or service developed at an appropriate price, promoted so customers find out about them and distributed in the most efficient way. They are responsible for the external-facing image of the company and how the company communicates. A lot of this activity is digital these days via websites and social media.

8. IT

Most companies have departments dedicated to IT whose responsibility is to maintain and operate any computer systems the company has. With the proliferation of computer systems for all aspects of a company, from sales and finance to recruitment, these departments have become very important with a large requirement for English.

9. Customer services

One of the fastest growing areas in most companies are help desks where customers can interact directly and get their queries answered. Although many companies outsource this activity, some look after it themselves. Customers can ask questions about their accounts, deliveries, purchases and so on. Good communication skills, patience and understanding are needed in this department.

10. Administration

Companies often have a department responsible for a wide range of administrative activities. They could be general services which all departments require, such as office supplies or vending machines, photocopiers or parking spaces. They could be responsible for archiving and use of the premises or a point of contact for annual returns which governments require. The precise function of the department will vary from country to country.

Unit 12

"My greatest concern was meeting the different expectations and needs of the students who wanted Business English for a wide range of sectors; marketing, meetings, presentations, in-company terms, project management and so on. I found I could suit most needs by adapting the material at hand."

Gillian Camilleri, Business English teacher, Malta

10 tips for planning a course

Most of your students, the training manager and your academic supervisor will expect you to have a plan for the course which shows the course content and activities planned to help you achieve the objectives that have been set. At the same time, you will need to be flexible and allow for things which were unknown at the start of the course to be covered. There will also be activities which prove more or less useful than others. You might also be supplied with published materials which have to be used within a needs-based course. All these factors make planning quite time consuming it is but well worth it once the course begins.

An example course plan is shown on p36.

1. Key facts

How many are in the group? What level are they? How long is the course going to be? What frequency are the lessons? What time of day? Is there a coursebook? Do I need to factor in testing? Will they do homework?

2. Individual needs

In any group there will be differing strengths, weaknesses, expectations and needs. On many Business English courses students are getting their only opportunity to learn English and want to take full advantage. A good activity in the first lesson is to ask everyone to write down their three main objectives for the course on large post-its and then place them on the whiteboard or flipchart and look for commonalities. They will use different words to express similar aims so you will need to do some editing. This will allow everyone to share their expectations publicly and see how a wide range of needs will need to be taken into consideration.

3. Optimise the classroom time

With a limited number of lessons you will need to use them to take full advantage of your presence. Activities where you are less useful can be done before or after class. Reading comprehension, vocabulary learning and practice, even listening can often be done ahead of the class so that you concentrate on production, correction and communication.

4. Coursebook

No coursebook is ever 100% perfect for any group and there is rarely time to complete every part of it. However, there are always a lot of useful activities which will save you huge amounts of time in preparation. One way to start a course is to look at the contents page as a class and see if any lessons look really useful in terms of the needs of the group. You could also do a unit in detail and discuss with the class how useful the various sections are. Some classes will expect you to teach them grammar, for example, but some coursebooks illustrate and explain grammar so well that students can often do those parts at home leaving the class for the communicative practice of the grammar.

5. Publish the plan

When you feel you have a workable plan for the course, let the class see it. It is important they see your percentages of the different skills, how you have covered their individual needs and how you have decided to use the coursebook. Make sure that individual requirements are covered at least twice. Include space in the plan for flexibility or for including lessons to revise or repeat areas where necessary.

6. Objectives

We have already discussed objectives, but it is important to reiterate that your plan must lead towards attainable objectives within the time allowed. Overambitious aims just mislead people. Language learning is very time intensive and there is only a certain amount which can be done, particularly when the average class will not be full of great linguists.

7. Student-centred activities

A percentage of any course (up to 25%) should be allocated to the class itself to manage. This can be in the form of peer teaching, with participants looking at particular vocabulary or grammar areas. It could also be in the form of them bringing in short reading texts or video clips to use as springboards for activities. Allow time for students to give presentations to the rest of the group because it's good, authentic practice which allows you, as the teacher, to take a back seat and assess progress.

8. Tutorials

One really useful slot to factor into your course is a tutorial. It only needs to be about 10 minutes long at a frequency you decide. While the group is working on a project or a case-study together, you take each participant aside for this time to chat with them, discuss the course, give them some individual praise and feedback.

9. Feedback

One of the hardest things to do is to get feedback on your teaching, but it is really key to the success of your course. More experienced teachers get feedback without explicitly asking but less experienced teachers need to ask the question. A simple activity is to look back at lessons and vote on their usefulness. Was it what the class needed? How useful will it be when they are back at work? Can they use that language or skill next week at their workplace? This sort of question will help you to refine your course and keep it closer to the route needed to meet the objectives.

10. Contract

A lot of trainers like to get participants to sign a contract. This is another way of getting learners to think about learning and also to think about being part of a learning group which they might not have been for quite a time. People are very sensitive, particularly when they are all from the same company, and the loud ones and the quiet ones both need to know what is expected. For example, using the mother tongue too often might lead to a fine. Not doing homework could have a similar result. Being late or not participating, being over critical or not listening are other aspects of a contract you might want to draw up and post on the wall or even post on a class Facebook page.

No course plan will look the same because it will be adapted according to the size and scope of the course and the client's needs. Here's an example of a course plan which has been designed for a five week course for a group of ten students from different departments. The class is described as B1, which is low intermediate. They meet twice a week for 120 minutes per lesson (20 hours in total).

Course Plan (May 28 – July 3)

Class:	Axxon 2
Level:	B1
Location:	Axxon training room

	Business topic	Language focus	Communication skill	Self study/ progress tests
Week 1	Your job and work routines	Present simple and present continuous Vocabulary: verbs for describing your responsibilities	Introducing yourself to others Making small talk	Online workbook Unit 1
Week 2	Telephoning	Pronunciation: spelling and numbers Grammar: determiners	Leaving a message Placing an order	Online workbook Unit 2
Week 3	Products and services	Adjectives for describing products and services Comparatives and superlatives	Presenting a product or service Preparing a short elevator pitch	Record and prepare your presentations
Week 4	Company profiles	Using pausing in presentations Video lesson: listening for key information and note-taking	Final presentations Give peer feedback	Online workbook Unit 3
Week 5	Systems in the workplace	Sequence language imperatives	Writing a list of instructions	Revise for progress test on July 3rd

10 ways to assess the students' language level

On most Business English courses you will be asked to report back regularly on the progress made by the class. The most useful way to do this is to regularly assess your students in ways which are not too formal, which do not take away valuable teaching time and which cover all the skills you are working on. By regularly noting down your scores and assessment you can be in a position to report on them. This list of activities covers most of the elements you will need to comment on.

1. Send them the same email and grade/compare their responses

Early on in the course, send each participant the same email asking for information about them, their job, the company and why they want to learn English. Their replies will give you valuable data about where they are in terms of level but also in terms of how they compare against each other. More detailed marking can look at specific areas such as tone, style, grammar, range of vocabulary, punctuation and so on.

2. Write a 100-word paragraph

Ask the class to write about a work-related topic in a 100-word paragraph. Your main question for this sort of writing is, 'Are they saying in English what they really want to say?', but at a more detailed level this piece of writing will tell you a lot about their level of grammar, vocabulary and writing.

3. Video record a two minute presentation

Like the first activity, recording a short presentation gives you a chance to have a snapshot of their English at any given time. Ideally you can do this at least three times during the course so that the students and you can notice any improvements. These improvements might be in confidence or self-correction or fluency. Avoid letting students use too many slides or visual aids in this kind of presentation, so that the focus is on their speaking.

4. Role play authentic oral situations

One of the key oral areas which needs to be assessed is how well people respond in typical communicative situations. Here you will be assessing how quickly they respond, how fluently they join in the conversation, how well they answer questions and take turns. This test can be set up by creating authentic work situations and having different groupings of two or three act them out. The situation can be on prompt cards and can cover situations like showing people around, asking for explanations, meeting a new member of staff, etc.

5. Who's calling?

If you cannot find the time to set up short face-to-face tests in class, you can always do them by telephone. This is in fact a very authentic way of assessing their listening and speaking skills and it is easy for you to stick to the same script for everyone, meaning that your assessment is based on the same original conversation. How clear they are, how they ask for clarification, how they respond to natural speech can all be assessed and recorded. You can ask them to take messages if you want to check further.

6. Listening skills

Adults struggle with listening, particularly when they are only studying English once a week. Try to persuade your students to listen for just ten minutes a day, then there will be a noticeable improvement; for example, they could listen to the BBC audio news which is available on the BBC website. You could set comprehension questions to check their level of understanding.

7. Common errors

If you regularly note down errors made in class and keep a record of them, they can be easily recycled into quick tests or quizzes. Hand out lists of sentences containing common errors and ask the class to correct them. Make sure you give extra marks to those who can explain why the mistake was made.

8. Vocabulary box

At the end of every lesson choose a dozen or so new words which the class want to add to their active vocabulary. Jot them on business card sized cards with either a definition or an example sentence on the reverse. Put these cards in a shoe-box and as the course progresses your vocabulary depository will grow. Every couple of weeks you can choose a dozen or so of the words for a vocabulary quiz/game. Students will soon realise that you are assessing their active vocabulary and will start to put in some more revision on their own. If the cardboard box is a little old-fashioned you can always use the digital equivalent.

9. Vocabulary cards

An extension of 8 is to distribute cards with key words on and encourage the class to introduce their words naturally into the conversation. Points are scored for using the words by steering the conversation in the direction required. This will give you a good idea of your students' conversational abilities.

10. Dictation

The assessment tool which requires little preparation but which is a very useful test is the dictation. You can use a text your class have never seen or a text they have, depending on what you are trying to achieve. Dictation is a good test of pronunciation, grammar, listening, vocabulary, spelling and writing.

"One of the ways that I get students to practise the language is by filming them speaking and then upload the videos on a private YouTube channel for self-assessment and peer-assessment."

Mardiana Idris, teacher, Malaysia

Read more about how Mardiana uses YouTube for assessment in her blog post at www.myetpedia.com.

Activities for business topics

Many courses base a lesson or series of lessons around a central business theme or topic. This is especially true if you are teaching pre-work students who are following a syllabus that looks at different areas of business. Equally, if you are working with in-work students in areas such as how to talk about graphs and charts, then you'll need some activities that activate the vocabulary or give the opportunity for speaking and discussion practice.

The aim of this section is to offer practical activities for a range of topics typically included on Business English courses. If you are following a Business English course book, you'll also find that many of the ideas here will support and supplement the content in the book.

Typically, each unit provides a series of ideas which start with lead-in discussion questions and activities you might do at the beginning of a lesson to introduce language and give controlled practice. Later activities in a unit tend to offer more opportunities for freer speaking practice and there is often a suggestion for some writing practice. Finally, note that even if you are not teaching a particular topic one week, you still might find an idea in the list for an activity that you can adapt to work with another topic.

10 activities for the topic of WORKPLACES and COMPANIES

All students need to be able to talk about the place where they work and their companies. There are a number of activities you can do to help practise the language of this topic. Remember that if you teach the students in their actual company premises, then take advantage of everything the workplace has to offer, from the physical environment itself to the activities which take place there.

1. Places of work

For a simple low-level introduction to the topic of workplaces, write the following workplaces on the board or adapt the list so you also include some of the workplaces that your own students work in.

1. School	2. Lorry	3. Office	4. Hospital	5. Showroom/Shop
6. University	7. Restaurant	8. Bank	9. Call centre	10. Laboratory

Ask students to work in pairs and write the job titles they might find working in each place. Note that there could be more than one answer. You could also set this up as a quiz between to two teams. Read out the place and each team guesses the job title to receive a point. After the exercise, ask students to talk about their own jobs and the places that they work in. (*Suggested answers: 1. teacher, 2. driver, 3. sales rep, 4. doctor/ nurse, 5. sales assistant, 6. lecturer, 7. waiter/chef, 8. cashier/manager, 9. telephonist/ call handler/operative, 10. scientist, researcher.*) Note that with very low level classes, you could write these answers in a second group on the board and students match them to the workplaces.

2. Product or service

This is another low level vocabulary exercise to start off a course or introduce the theme of company types. Write a selection of company types on the board, for example: *Finance, Vehicle manufacturer, Legal, Energy, Pharmaceutical, Fashion, Education*. Make sure students know the difference between the terms *Products* or *Services*. Ask them to categorise the types of companies into the two groups: group 1 = companies which make products, group 2 =companies which provide services. You could also ask them to think of examples of real companies they know and make sentences such as: *HSBC is a finance company which provides banking services*. End the activity with students making sentences about their own company, saying what type of company it is and whether it makes products or provides services.

3. Organograms

If you have covered the language presented in 1 and 2, or you are working with higher level students, you could start to use an organogram. This is a graphic showing the organisation or structure of a team, department or company. If you are working for large companies, they probably have one to refer to. Otherwise, ask your students to draw one, or do your own research and create one. If you teach pre-work students then they could find one for a company by searching online.

Show the class the organogram and introduce phrases such as *deal with, be in charge of, be responsible for, head up, work with/for/under* by explaining the structure and who is responsible for what. Then ask students questions such as *'Who is in charge of sales?'* or *'Which department reports to the finance director?'*. Next put students in pairs and they take turns to ask and answer questions in the same way.

You could also use the photocopiable activity on p146. Make one copy of the page for two students and cut the page in half. Put students in pairs and given them the A/B copies of the organogram. They take turns to ask each other for the missing information using questions such as *'Who is in charge of …?'*, *'Who reports to ...?'*, *'Who is responsible for...?'*, etc.

4. Presenting your company

As a follow-on activity to the previous activities, ask students to prepare visuals of their own department or team and a brief presentation for homework. They can then give the presentation to the class in the next lesson. As well as providing a very useful lexical set, the activity recycles present tenses and gives students the chance to make a simple presentation whatever their level of English.

5. Talking about locations

With lower level classes, introduce the names of different departments and parts of the building and then teach prepositions of place (e.g. *next to, opposite, between, above,* etc.). Then they practise talking about different parts of the building or place they work in and where things are.

You can also make copies of the floor plans on p147. Students work in pairs and receive a copy of the floor plan with different location names missing. They take turns to ask each other about the missing place names and write them in. The person answering will need to use prepositions of place. For example:

Student A: *'What is on the left of the general manager's office?'*

Student B: *'The conference room.'*

Note that if you have a copy of the students' actual company floor plan you can turn it into a similar information gap activity.

6. Giving directions

Following on from the activity in 5, another useful in-company skill is to give directions to visitors using language such as *'Go straight down this corridor, turn left, stop outside the …,'* etc. If you have a map of the company you are working in then use this as the basis for a speaking activity. Students can work in pairs and take turns to give each other directions around the map. You could also use the floor plan on p147. Student A imagines they are standing in the car park. Student B gives them directions to an unnamed room in the building. Student A listens and guesses which location Student B has given directions to.

7. Workplace videos

Get your students to make short videos with English narration about an aspect of their company using the video recorder on a smartphone or tablet. (Note that you need to make sure you have permission and to state you are not going to be putting the videos into the public domain.) Put students in pairs or groups and ask them to make a two-minute film about an aspect of the workplace. This could be a report about the canteen, a short documentary on a process, an interview with a colleague or even a welcome video. Allow plenty of time for planning the script before students start filming and set aside classroom times for students to present their final efforts.

8. Rules and regulations

Many workplaces have a number of rules and regulations which need to be illustrated and explained to new starters and visitors. One way to do an activity on this topic is to write some rules on the board, such as:

▶ *Employees must wear a security badge at all times.*

▶ *All staff have to wear a uniform.*

▶ *Visitors cannot enter the building unless accompanied by a member of staff.*

Students work on their own or in pairs and decide which of the rules are true for their workplace and which need to be rewritten. This activity is a good follow-up to a lesson on modals of obligation (*must, have to, cannot,* etc.). At higher levels a little humour can be introduced with some unofficial rules being introduced or some non-rules such as *'Employees should feel happy at all times'*.

9. Key numbers and figures

All Business English students need basic numbers practice in English and even higher level students can struggle when saying bigger numbers. So before the next lesson, ask students to find out five key numbers and figures related to their company. For example: annual turnover, monthly production, number of employees, units sold, number of overseas offices, etc. Then they bring their numbers to the next lesson. Put the students in pairs and they practise dictating the numbers to a partner or to the rest of the class, who writes them down. One variation is to have students say a number and the rest of the class has to guess what it refers to; e.g. is it the annual turnover or the number of people employed? You can also introduce questions forms such as:

How much ...?, How many ...?, What percentage ...?, etc. and students take turns to ask and answer questions about the company.

10. Company website reading comprehension

For companies with a website containing information about the business, you can prepare sets of comprehension questions and students have to search for the answers on the website. Students can also prepare their own questions for each other by looking for key information on their company's website and writing questions. Ideally, this is done with students working in pairs and then they swap their questions with another pair. In-work students can write questions based on their own company's website or perhaps a competitor. Pre-work students could be allocated different well-known companies to research and then prepare questions for each other.

10 activities for the topic of MARKETING and ADVERTISING

Most companies employ people to market and promote their products, services and brands. Note that pre-work students may need your help with some of the theoretical side of marketing as well as doing some practical language work. Although not everyone in your class is necessarily directly involved in marketing, they will be interested in the subject from a consumer's point of view.

1. Discussion questions

Lead into the lesson by writing these types of questions on the board and asking students to discuss them as a class, in pairs or in small groups:

How much do adverts affect what you buy?

Which kinds of adverts attract your attention?

Where does your company advertise itself?

How important is the company website in marketing?

2. Defining a product launch

The aim of this activity is to map all the stages from an initial idea through to the launch of a new product or service. First of all, list the key stages on the board, including:

Research and development.

Market research.

Conceptualisation.

Costing.

Prototyping.

Testing.

Naming.

Promotion.

Launch.

Put students in pairs and ask them to prepare one sentence which describes what happens at each stage. They can refer to dictionaries for useful words if necessary. At the end, ask different pairs to read their definitions until you have a complete description of the process.

3. Planning a product launch

As a follow-on to activity 2, students now plan a product launch. Ask the class to choose a product or service. If all your students work in a specialised sector like pharmaceuticals then you can choose a new drug or other form of treatment, whereas if you have a mixed group (or a pre-work class) you might want to choose something more familiar to everyone, like a chocolate bar or a perfume.

The class should decide what product or service you are going to launch and for which market and segment (age, status, current customers, etc.). Students then break out into groups and plan the name, the product description, the price, the promotional campaign and a slogan. Groups have half an hour to prepare a presentation with visual aids if necessary. After the presentations have been given, students can vote on the best plan.

ETpedia: 500 ideas for Business English teachers © Pavilion Publishing and Media Ltd and its licensors 2016.

Unit 16

4. Collocation pelmanism

This activity helps activate vocabulary with a focus on marketing related collocations. Prepare cards (about the size of business cards) with one word from each collocation below. You will need to have enough cards to have 28 per group of four students.

Market research	Advertising campaign	Product launch
Free sample	End user	Marketing director
Market share	Press release	Advertising hoardings
Target market	Brand stretching	Customer feedback
Mail shot	Special offer	

Students work in groups of four with the 28 cards facing down on the table. They play pelmanism by turning over two cards at a time trying to find a pair which make a collocation. If someone finds a pair they need to make a perfect sentence using the collocation in order to keep the pair. They keep going until they make a mistake and the next player has a turn. You will also find a photocopiable set of the cards with these collocations on p148. Note that some words will collocate with more than one so there might be multiple answers in some cases; for example *target market* and *target customer* are both correct.

5. Market your class/school

This activity works at any level and uses the knowledge people have of marketing, either because that is their work area or as an end-user. It is very simple in terms of preparation and usually generates a lot of language. Begin by telling the class that your school needs to get more customers for the following year. You have been briefed to decide on the marketing strategy which will reach and inform more potential customers about your services. Brainstorm ideas and elicit these main areas:

▶ Website   ▶ Marketing event   ▶ Trade-fair   ▶ Flyers
▶ Products courses ▶ Offers   ▶ Competitions   ▶ Sponsorship

Divide the class into groups of four and distribute two or three subjects to each group to brainstorm more ideas. Provide them with a whiteboard or flipchart to work with. Encourage them to write their ideas on post-its and place them next to the topic. After a few minutes the groups move on and brainstorm the next idea adding to the previous group's post-its. Repeat this until everyone has talked about all topics and then decide as a group three or four to concentrate on. Each group then takes one of the chosen subjects and works on a detailed plan. The final task is to present each area to the rest of the class and ideally arrive at a useful marketing plan for your school.

6. Logos

As a fun lead in to the topic of company logos, make copies of some logos but remove any full names so that you only have the symbols. Show the symbols and students have to guess the company. You could also turn it into a team competition with different teams receiving points for every logo they recognise. Note that if you photocopy logos in black and white, you can make the task more difficult with students trying to remember what colours are used in the logo. As a follow up, students can be given fictional businesses in different sectors and asked to design and then present new logos.

7. Slogans

As with the previous activity, you can also write company slogans on the board and students have to guess which company uses the slogan. Once you have looked at some examples of slogans and discussed which ones are more memorable than others, put students in groups and have them write a slogan. Another alternative is to give each group a different photograph and tell them that it is going to be used in advert. For example, it might be a photograph of a child's toy. The group has to write a slogan to appear with the photograph in a magazine advert.

8. Adverts around the classroom

Adverts in magazines or from the internet provide a rich source of interesting and authentic texts. Choose a selection of adverts and pin them around the room. You can design comprehension questions such as, 'Which advert is aimed at customers aged over 60?' Many adverts also contain comparative and superlative forms so a useful grammar lesson is for students to walk around, read the adverts and make notes of any examples they find.

9. Improving advertising copy

Show students the following text. Explain that it is advertising a new type of packaged ready-to-cook meals but that the words in bold don't make the product sound exciting. Students read the text and, working pairs, think of interesting words to replace those in bold. There is no one correct answer, so students should share their ideas afterwards.

*Have you tried our **nice** new range of ready-to-cook vegetarian meals? They're really **good**. You just take them out of the **cardboard** packet and heat them up. They look **good** and everyone in your family will **like** eating them.*

(Possible replacement words: *exciting, tasty, colourful, delicious, love.*)

10. Writing advertising copy

As a follow-on to activity 9, choose an area which will be of interest to your class, such as tourist attractions, hotels or restaurants. Find some examples of website copy where they are being promoted and print them off for the class to look at. Find examples in the texts of adjectives and adverbs often used in advertising, such as *stunning, mouth-watering, state-of-the-art*, etc. and write them on the board to pre-teach. Ask the class to scan the various texts looking for them. When they have understood the role of such adjectives, ask them to work in pairs to write promotional sentences for their office, their colleagues, their gadgets, etc. Finally, ask your students to write a short paragraph describing, in the most glowing terms, something or somewhere they would like to promote – a village, a shop or a local landmark for example.

10 activities for the topic of SALES

Although sales has historically been considered a specialist activity, a widespread belief these days is that everybody in the company is a potential salesperson. Every contact you have with the outside world is an opportunity to represent the values and services of your company and thus to either increase or decrease the chances of future business depending on how you behave. Here are 10 activities to explore the language and concepts of sales.

1. Discussion questions

What was the last thing you bought?

Why did you buy it?

How much did someone influence your decision to buy it?

What have you sold this week?

'A good salesman can sell a bad product but a good product sells itself.' Discuss.

2. Qualities of a top salesperson

Ask the class to brainstorm the qualities of a good sales person. Ideas they will probably come up with include:

▶ Knowledgeable about the product

▶ Persuasive

▶ Good with numbers

▶ Charming

▶ Persistent

▶ A good listener

▶ Pleasant

▶ Hard-working

▶ Competitive

▶ Loyal

When you have a list of 10 or so ideas ask them to work in pairs and to rank the six most important qualities from most to least important. At higher levels ask them to give examples to justify their ranking.

3. Quotes

There are many sayings and quotes about selling and you can find lots online. For example, here are the first five listed on a website called http://senatorclub.co/101-greatest-sales-quotes-of-all-time/.

1. 'To me, job titles don't matter. Everyone is in sales. It's the only way we stay in business.'
   – Harvey Mackay

2. 'Remember that failure is an event, not a person. Yesterday ended last night.'
   – Zig Ziglar

3. 'Pretend that every single person you meet has a sign around his or her neck that says, "Make me feel important." Not only will you succeed in sales, you will succeed in life.'
   – Mary Kay Ash

4. 'If you are not taking care of your customer, your competitor will.'
   – Bob Hooey

5. 'Sales are contingent upon the attitude of the salesman, not the attitude of the prospect.'
   – William Clement Stone

Quotes like these are useful not only because of their content, which makes for good discussions, but also as good models for pronunciation. The quotes are often structured to make an impact during a presentation or speech so they often contain useful examples of some of the keys to English pronunciation such as rhythm, intonation, stress, linking and pausing.

Copy them on to strips of paper and distribute to individuals. Get one student at a time to read out their quote in a dramatic, inspiring way for the others to jot down.

4. Communicative crossword

A good way of recycling vocabulary you have taught during a number of lessons is to turn a list of words into a crossword with both horizontal and vertical clues. (You will find lots of free-to-use online tools which make crosswords by searching for 'crossword makers') To create an activity, fill in two versions of the crossword, one with horizontal words completed and one with vertical ones. Students work in pairs and receive one version of the crossword. They take turns to give their partner a clue for a word in their crossword and the partner has to guess it. See the ready-to-use photocopiable crossword with words related to sales on p150.

5. Features and benefits

A key part of selling is to be able to differentiate between the features and the benefits of a product. A **feature** is what the product has, such as a protective cover in the case of a tablet, and the **benefit** is what this does for the customer (stops the screen getting damaged). The benefit is one of the main drivers for a customer to purchase a product because it helps them solves a problem they have. A good salesman can show features, benefits and advantages of a product to a particular customer. A simple activity is to give out cards with the name of a product on, e.g. blue-tooth speaker, ironing board, pencil case, flash-drive, etc. The students have to write down a list of features, benefits and advantages and present to a partner.

6. A sales pitch

Part of any lesson on sales will include students trying to sell something. An easy way to do this is to bring in a collection of any objects and hand them out randomly. Students need to look at their object and prepare a sales pitch in which they will list its benefits to the end-user. Monitor and help students by providing words they need. When everyone's ready, students work in pairs and take turns to try and sell their object to their partner. Set a time limit of two minutes for the sales pitch. At the end, ask students to comment on which partners were convincing and to say what makes a good sales pitch.

7. Elevator pitch

A variation or extension to the activity in 6 is for students to give an elevator pitch. The idea of an elevator pitch is based on the apocryphal story of someone who got into the lift at the same time as one of the senior managers and had only the time in the lift (elevator) to present his ideas. Apparently it worked.

The aim is to present a compelling sales pitch for someone or something in a very short space of time (30–60 seconds). Students can either be selling an object as in the previous activity or they can imagine they are in the elevator with the CEO of a company and they want to get a promotion, so they sell themselves. Give them time to prepare their pitch which should be clear, persuasive, quantifiable and interesting, lasting no more than one minute. To succeed the student needs to have good language and body language as well as being convincing. You can draw up a score-sheet covering varying aspects such as engagement, vocabulary, fluency, eye contact and so on and then have the class deliver their pitches with everyone else judging. (See also a photocopiable version on p149.) Search YouTube for some excellent examples of elevator pitches.

8. Dialogue building

After-sales is another area you might look at connected to this topic, and how to handle complaints is useful for many students. With lower level learners, build up a dialogue as a class. Explain that Student A is the person listening and Student B is complaining. Decide if the complaint is over the telephone, in a shop or in a hotel. Ask the class what A's opening question could be, for example:

A *How can I help you?*

Practise the line then elicit the response.

B *I'd like to return this pullover.*

Practise both lines around the class before adding the next line

A *Could you tell me what the problem is?*

Continue the same method of adding lines and practising until you have around 8–10 lines. Students practise in pairs before changing some of the content to make a new dialogue including expressions like '*I do apologise*', '*I'll see what we can do*', '*No problem*', '*Thank you for your patience*', etc. Final versions can be recorded on their smartphones. Get learners to pay particular attention to intonation, which is very important in these situations.

9. Negotiating expressions

A good activity with larger classes which encourages negotiation is a shortened version of Monopoly. Divide the class into six groups and then distribute the property cards from the board game equally as if you were playing cards. Then give each group £1000 to spend. They have to buy and sell properties in order to end up with complete sets they can build houses and hotels on. Give them ten minutes to negotiate by moving around the room. The winning group will have the best combination of cash and full sets of properties. Monitor the language used and correct and add where necessary. Students should use language like *If I give you Mayfair, will you give me two stations? How much would I need to give you for Park Lane?*

10. Customer feedback forms

Companies asking customers for feedback has become commonplace, especially with online retailers such as Amazon. Show students examples of these types of feedback forms or online surveys and then ask them to design one either for their own products or services or perhaps for a product they have been reading about, or something fictional. They could create their feedback forms using an online tool such as SurveyMonkey which allows you to post a questionnaire online for others to answer.

This topic covers a broad range of jobs and activities. A number of people working in these areas often use English in written forms rather than spoken, which means they often have knowledge of grammar and vocabulary which needs to be activated. The pre-work learner, on the other hand, will need activities which help them learn about finance and English together.

1. Finance quiz

To introduce the theme of money and finance, start your lesson with a quiz. Divide the group up into two to four teams and explain that each of them is going to create a quiz for the others. They have to come up with 10 questions following this sort of template.

1. A picture question, e.g. Where is this coin from?

2. A currency question, e.g. What is the currency of Thailand?

3. A history question, e.g. When was the euro launched?

4. A language question, e.g. How do you pronounce this word – *debt*?

5. A value question, e.g. What is the most expensive painting ever sold?

6. A music question, e.g Complete this title: _____ *can't buy me love.*

7. An anagram, e.g. Make a word from these letters: LLMNRIIEOAI.

8. A film question, e.g. Complete this title. *The Wolf of _____.*

9. A geography question, e.g Where is Fort Knox?

10. An expression/idiom question, e.g. If you tighten your _____ you will spend less money.

You can do this example quiz as practice and to give them an idea of the kind of questions to ask. Allow them access to books and the internet to find information. All of the questions need to be written out then you can organise the quiz as question-master. You could also offer chocolate money as prizes. See a photocopiable version of this quiz on page 151.

2. Create a quiz

As a follow-up to the quiz in activity 1, ask students to work in small groups and create their own quiz. This will require some research and access to the internet so it could worth allowing time at home for preparing it. Then students share their quizzes and test each other.

3. Number dictations

All language learners struggle with numbers, and people in finance probably need more practice than most. Learners need to be able to both understand and say numbers in clear, confident English. Numbers said hesitantly do not create the right impression in an international meeting. A simple warmer is to give a large number to one student who repeats it once only to the next student who repeats it to the next student and so on around the room. Quick arithmetical dictations are useful practice as well. You say '20% of 15' and the class write down '3'. Bingo also works and takes minimal preparation. Students write down eight numbers between, say, 101 and 199, and as you read out numbers they tick them off. The winner is first to tick of all their numbers.

4. Matching foreign exchanges to countries

A nice finance based activity for looking at nationalities and countries is to bring in a map of the world along with luggage tags with the names of well-known financial exchange indices such as Nikkei (Japan), FTSE (UK), CAC 40 (France), IBOVESPA (Brazil). Students take a tag and place it on the map. If they are not sure they can take advice from their colleagues. There are a large number of these indices which you can find on any financial websites like Google Finance or BBC Finance.

5. Finance headlines

Using real financial news stories from around the world provides a lot of useful general financial vocabulary. One way to begin is to print off a sheet with seven or eight stories and remove the headlines. Students can either match the headline to the news story or write their own headlines and match them with the originals.

6. Scanning the news

As a follow-up to activity 5, use the same news stories but this time prepare comprehension questions which require students to locate the answer quickly by scanning the whole page. To add movement and interest, pin the news stories on the walls of your classroom so students have to move around to find the answers. One variation is for students to prepare their own questions as a follow-up.

7. Exchange rate pairwork

An authentic activity which uses up-to-date information is to swap exchange rates or any other financial information such as commodity prices or stock exchange indices which you can find on financial websites or in the financial press. Students each find five different exchange rates via a website such as http://www.xe.com and then simulate a phone call exchanging the information.

8. Connect four

This vocabulary activity is a way to recycle and review recently taught vocabulary. First of all, demonstrate the activity by writing the following 16 words randomly around the board: *pay, sell, purchase, borrow, cash, cheque, card, transfer, bank, ATM, post office, currency exchange office, fall, rise, decline, fluctuate.* Ask students to connect the sets of four words and name the category. The four categories are: financial verbs, ways of paying, locations for money, and financial trends. Next, give four post-it notes or pieces of paper to each student and ask them to write four different words on them that are connected in some way. After all the students have written their four words, they put their words randomly around on the board or spread around a table. Then, the students must decide which words are connected and name the category. Note that this activity can easily be adapted for many other business topics.

9. Lemonade stall

With a pre-work class you could use this excellent simulation which is used in secondary schools and is available for free at http://www.coolmath-games.com/. The aim is to run a successful stand selling lemonade over a period of time, minimum seven days. The class know what the weather forecast is for each day and have to decide how much lemonade they will sell and at what price. They have to buy the ingredients (lemons, sugar, ice) and the cups and try to get a good price. The aim is to make the largest profit possible each day. The game automatically generates discussion, hypotheses, guessing, trial and error and many other business strategies, all in English. Key vocabulary like *raw materials, gross profit, net price, discount*, will be used on a regular basis. The website also has a similar simulation about running a coffee shop.

10. Budget roleplays

Most coursebooks have some activities based on finance, often a role play in which students have to discuss how to allocate budgets. A minimalist way of setting up such an activity is to announce to the class that their company of 100 people has been left $20,000 by a former employee but that the money has to be spent making life easier for the staff. You can get the class to make suggestions or supply them with these ideas:

Refurbish canteen: $12,000

Build a small cinema: $20,000

Create a roof terrace: $15,000

Organise a party: $6,000

Dinner, show and hotel in the capital: $20,000

Arrange barbecue for staff and families: $3,000

Buy minibus: $20,000

Employ part-time personal trainer: $200 per week

Students work in small groups and come to a decision as to how to spend the money. They can then prepare a short explanation of their plans for the larger class to discuss. The class will then decide on which options to take up.

Unit 18

10 activities for the topic of CULTURE

In Business English, the topic of culture is often inseparable from many other topics and activities that your students might be involved in, after all, your students are learning English in order to communicate with people from different cultures. Of course, the term 'culture' can be hard to define as it might refer to national cultures or it can also refer to company culture and management styles. These 10 activities explore both types.

1. Questions about culture

Whenever the topic of culture comes up in a lesson, for example in a reading text or when watching a video about the way people do something in a different culture, always follow it up by asking students questions such as: *Is this also true in your country? How is it different in your country? How would you do this in your country?* Remember that lessons about cultural differences should always include the students reflecting on their own culture as well as those of others.

2. Do's and don'ts

There are lots of books and websites dedicated to the topic of what you should or shouldn't do when you visit another country with strong cultural differences. For example, they'll tell you that in one country you're expected to be late for dinner at someone's house whereas in another country you should be very punctual. Sometimes these kinds of rules aren't 100% true but they make a useful starting point into the topic. For example, here are five tips on having meetings with business people from China.

- ▶ Meetings start on time. Be punctual.
- ▶ You'll probably shake hands, but sometimes people will also bow slightly.
- ▶ Everyone should receive your business card.
- ▶ Silence is often expected in a meeting. Don't interrupt immediately.
- ▶ Be prepared to wait. You don't normally get a quick final decision.

Ask students to read them and say if they are true in their country. If you teach Chinese students you could even ask them how correct they are.

3. Write your own rules

Once students have read a list of do's and don'ts like the ones in activity 2, ask them to write their own rules or rewrite the rules so they are true for their own country. If students come from the same country, they could do this working in pairs. Note that this activity can also work well if you link it with verbs for giving rules, such as *have to, must, are not allowed, can't* e.g. *You must arrive on time for formal meetings*.

4. Which rule is false?

As a variation to the activity in 3, you can add some fun by saying to the students they should write three or four rules about culture in their country but make one of the rules untrue. Then they read the rules to their partner who must guess which rule is made up. For example:

A: In my country, you have to take your shoes and socks off before entering someone's office.

B: I think that's false!

5. Food on a menu

The topic of food is always of interest to students and especially useful for business students who eat out a lot when visiting other countries. This activity involves students creating an international cross-cultural menu. Begin by asking students to name the different parts of a menu and write them on the board. Answers may vary slightly, but you should get titles like *starters, main course, dessert*

Put students into groups of three. (If you have a class of students from different cultures then make sure each group contains students from different cultural backgrounds.) Explain that the students are going to open a hotel restaurant for international business people. They must create a menu which is going to satisfy every type of cultural background. As students discuss the different dishes they will need to discuss what is in each dish and how it's made. They should make notes and if you have time, they can even write up their menu for everyone to read.

6. Routines

Many coursebooks, especially at lower levels, include a reading or listening about someone's daily routine; e.g. *I get up at 7, I eat toast for breakfast, I start work at 8.30. My weekend is on Saturday and Sunday.* If you come across this kind of text, then ask students to say what is different about their routine or even to write a short paragraph about it. Daily routines in different countries are not always the same so it can be useful to draw attention to these simple differences.

7. Company culture

Discussing company culture can be sensitive because you want students to talk about the culture of their own companies. This might be a problem if everyone is from the same company and from different levels of management. However, it's an interesting discussion topic if introduced sensitively. Write the following sentences on the board and ask students to score each sentence on a scale between 1 and 5. 1 = Not true for my company, 5 = Very true for my company.

1. *Employees are often asked for their opinions and ideas.*
2. *The management structure is fairly flat.*
3. *Everyone talks and socialises with each other.*
4. *Meetings are usually informal and friendly.*
5. *People are allowed to break rules.*

Afterwards, students compare their scores. Note that high scores indicate a student's company has a relaxed culture with a flat structure. Point out that a low score is not necessarily bad, but indicates a more hierarchical company culture, which may be more appropriate for a certain type of business. Allow time for students to compare their scores. Encourage them to explain their answers and what they say about the company culture.

8. The relocation

When people relocate with the same company but to other parts of the world, they often receive some kind of induction on arrival so that they become familiar with the culture of their new country and also the local company culture. Put students into groups and explain that a new person from a different region is relocating for two years. The groups must plan a two-day induction which includes finding out about the company culture and also introducing them to different aspects of their country's culture. Each group prepares an itinerary and then presents it to the class.

9. Critical incidents

Critical incidents are descriptions of situations where a problem occurs in a business situation and students have to speculate what the cause of the problem is. You will find many examples of these online by searching with the words *Cultural Critical Incidents*. For example, here is an example of a critical incident: *A German business person has to telephone his colleague in the UK once a week. His English colleague always starts the phone conversation by asking him about his week, the weather and his family. This irritates the German but he is too polite not to answer all his colleague's questions. What's the problem?*

Put students in small groups and ask them to discuss what they think is going wrong here and how it might be avoided in the future. One possible explanation might be: *In England it's typical to start off a conversation with plenty of small talk and questions about general topics before getting down to business. In Germany, however, it's more common to quickly get down to business.*

10. Business ethics

This final activity is based around the topic of business ethics but it has an interesting cultural dimension because students in a class from different cultures might sometimes view ethical issues differently according to their cultural background. Write the list below on the board and ask your students to rank them from 1 to 8 (1=most unethical, 8=least unethical).

▶ Multinational companies paying very small rates of tax.

▶ Unequal pay for men and women.

▶ A family member or friend being promoted because of their connection (known as *nepotism*).

▶ The glass ceiling for female employees.

▶ Pharmaceutical companies not giving free medicine to poor countries.

▶ Former politicians earning huge salaries from corporations.

▶ Young children in developing countries working long hours on low (or no) pay to produce clothes for export to developed countries.

▶ Placing sweets at supermarket checkout points to attract children.

Then put students into groups and have them present and explain their choices. Groups should try to agree upon the same order by the end of their discussion.

10 activities for the topic of GRAPHS and CHARTS

Strictly speaking, graphs and charts aren't really a topic but they regularly appear in different business contexts. They often appear in business reading texts, students need to include and refer to them when writing reports, and presenters talk about them on their slides. Students need to know how to understand the vocabulary of graphs and charts, how to use the vocabulary of trend language, and to explain the reasons for results.

1. Types of graphs and charts

Establish the different types of visual that we often use to show results. You can easily do this by showing examples, ideally taken from the students' own materials. Alternatively, sketch these drawings on the board and write the words below. Students match a-f to the sketches 1-6. (Answers: 1b, 2e, 3a, 4f, 5d, 6c)

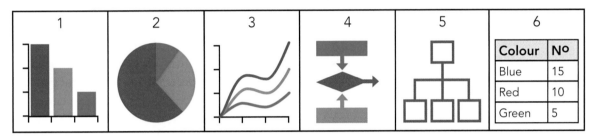

a. graph	b. bar chart	c. table
d. organogram	e. pie chart	f. flowchart

2. Using graphs and charts

If your students are unfamiliar with the way that some of the charts and graphs in activity 1 are used (which might be true for many pre-work students), then write the following six types of results on the board and students must decide which graph or chart would be most suitable to show the results.

A. Structure of the divisions in a multinational.

B. Different populations in five different countries.

C. Results from a survey of customers.

D. Comparison of two sets of sales figures over the last five years.

E. Diagram of a process for taking customer enquiries.

F. Market share in different regions.

(Suggested answer, although students might be able to justify variations: A5, B1, C6, D3, E4, F2)

3. Matching graphs and charts to the text

In the financial sections of the business news you'll often find different graphs and charts in one article and different parts of the text refers to each one – *The Economist* magazine is particularly useful for this. Separate the graph and charts and mix them up on one page. Then put the text on another page. The task is for students to read the text and decide which graph or chart is being referred to.

Unit 20

4. Trend language

Write a selection of trend language on the board, like this:

Increase	Fall	Rise	Stay the same	Go Up
Decrease	Remain steady	Go down	Level off	Reach a peak

Next, ask students to indicate the direction of the trend for each word with these symbols:
↑ ↓ →

(Answers: increase ↑   fall ↓   rise ↑   stay the same →   go up ↑
decrease ↓   remain steady →   go down ↓   level off →   reach a peak ↑)

5. Reading for trend language

Following on from the idea of using a text with lots of graphs and charts in activity 3 and the idea of indicating the movement of trend language in activity 4, it's also helpful to find texts with trend language in and have students underline any of the trend words or phrases. They then transfer the new language to their vocabulary notes and add one of the arrows ↑ ↓ → next to it for future reference. They should also add other information such as whether the word is a verb or noun; e.g. to increase (v), an increase (n).

6. Describing trends on graphs

For this activity you need students to have the same graph but with different trend lines on. You might be able to find such a graph and edit it or you could create one. (See also a photocopiable version on p152.) The two students are each given a different version of the same graph. Student A describes his/her trend line on the graph and Student B copies it on his/hers. Then they swap roles and Student B describes the trend line with Student A copying. Afterwards, they compare the trend lines to see if they are correct.

7. Writing descriptions of trends

As an alternative to the speaking activity in 6, you could ask students to write their descriptions of the trend line and then swap their writing with a partner who reads the description and draws the trend line onto the graph. Alternatively, choose a graph that may be of interest to a student or relevant to their job and have them write a paragraph about it.

8. Describing reasons for trends and results

In presentations, students often need to explain the reason for a trend. You will need to pre-teach the language of cause and effect in **bold**: *There was an increase in employment **because of/as a result of/due to** foreign investment in the region.*

Next, read out the following results and ask students to write them down.

▶ *UK ice cream sales fall between October and March.*

▶ *Energy prices stay the same over the summer.*

▶ *The cost of pensions for the government is increasing.*

Next, students work in pairs or small groups and have to speculate on possible reasons for each result using the language of cause and effect. As well as thinking of obvious reasons such as *UK ice cream sales fall between October and March* **because of** *the colder weather* students could also try to think of other possibilities. At the end, ask each group to present and compare their different ideas for the reasons.

9. Presenting graphs and charts

As a final culmination to all the work done on this language topic, ask students to bring in a graph or chart relevant to their own job and prepare a short presentation which makes use of it. At the end, the other students could ask them questions about the visual aids, for example, asking for the reasons for certain results.

10. Screen capture the presentation

As an alternative to activity 9, students could record their presentations of a graph or chart and send it to you for homework. They will need to use some kind of screen capture technology that allows you to copy the graph or chart on the screen of your laptop and record your voice describing it. There are a number of online tools that will do this for you including Jing, Snagit, Brainshark or Present.me.

"I often get asked what my favourite technology is and it is probably one of the few questions about technology that I find easy to answer. For me, there is nothing like screen capture technology. It is so versatile, easy to use and can be used in so many different ways that I really don't know what I would do if I didn't have access to it."

Russell Stannard, Educational Technologist, UK

Read more about how Russell uses screen capture technology at www.myetpedia.com and his website www.teachertrainingvideos.com

10 activities for the topic of APPLYING FOR A JOB

Most Business English courses will include at least one lesson on the topic of applying for a job. In fact, on courses aimed at pre-work students who will need to apply for positions in the future, it's useful to spend a series of lessons looking at the type of skills and language they will need.

1. Brainstorm the steps

Introduce students to the topic of applying for a job by writing the words 'You need a job' at the top of the board and 'You get the job' at the bottom of the board. Put students into pairs or small groups and ask them to brainstorm all the steps in between to get from needing a job to getting a job. If there is time, students could create flowcharts between the two ends of applying for a job. Their ideas might include a whole range of different steps including: *deciding what type of job you want, getting the right qualification, creating a CV, looking at job vacancies, approaching companies, going for an interview, getting rejected, going for another interview*, etc. Groups could present and share their lists to each other before you bring all the ideas together as a class.

2. Which are the synonyms?

While working on this topic, students will come across a number of words with a similar meaning (synonyms). You could introduce some of this vocabulary in the following way. Write the words on the board in groups of three (without the underlining). Students have to identify which two words are synonyms and which word is the odd one out. The underlined words are the synonyms:

position, job, interview

advert, CV, resumé

applicant, employer, candidate

hire, recruit, fire

qualifications, interests, education

salary, cost, pay

hours, duties, responsibilities

3. Personal qualities

When applying for jobs, students will need to use adjectives and nouns to describe their personal qualities, for example in their CV, application form or when describing themselves at an interview. Write a selection of personal quality words on the board which can be used to describe people, such as *flexible, hard-working, careful, dynamic, creative, enthusiastic, a teamworker, motivated, decisive, a self-starter, reliable*, etc. Begin by playing a game in which you define each of the words starting with the words '*It's someone who is …*' The idea is that students work in small groups and take turns to say a sentence like, '*It's someone who is able to change and work in different ways*'. The other students look at the list on the board and guess the word '*flexible*'. To prepare their definitions, you could give students time to look up the words in a dictionary and write their sentences. As they practise, make sure they can pronounce each of the words correctly so that they can use them in a job interview situation.

4. Ranking qualities

As a follow-up to the activity in 3, leave a selection of personal quality words on the board and give students a job title such as 'manager', 'IT programmer', 'teacher', 'nurse', etc. For each job title, ask students to rank the personal quality words in order of importance for the job with the first being the most important and the last being the least important or not important at all. This simple activity is a good way to get students thinking which of their own personal qualities will be important for the job they want to get.

5. Creating job adverts

Although many students will never have to write job adverts (unless they plan on working in the areas of human resources and recruitment), it's a useful exercise as it helps them to learn the type of vocabulary they might need during the process of applying for a job. One way to introduce the vocabulary is to bring in a selection of job adverts taken from newspapers or recruitment sites on the internet. Pin these around the room, then ask students to stand up, walk around and make a list of all the information given in each advert. For example, many adverts will include: *job title and responsibilities, location, name of employer, qualifications and personal qualities required, salary, contact details.* Once your students have created a list of items to include, ask them to think of a job they would really like to apply for in the future. Tell them to create an advert for the job. They could write it as though a real company has advertised it or they can create an imaginary employer. It might not even be a real job, or perhaps it's their 'dream' job (e.g. a rock star, a TV celebrity etc.) The main aim is that they produce an advert which includes all the features they listed. The writing could be done working on their own or in pairs. As they write, they could use any useful phrases or vocabulary that they came across in the adverts you pinned around the room.

6. What makes an effective CV?

As with the job adverts in 5, if you need to teach CV writing skills, it's helpful to bring in sample CVs and have students analyse what information is included. Note that in different countries CVs can vary in format so students will need to adjust theirs depending on where they are applying. Once students have studied example CVs, ask them to work in groups and draw up a list of what makes an effective CV. Afterwards, they compare their lists with other groups'.

7. Write in the missing sub-headings

Many CVs include sub-headings such as 'Qualifications', 'Interests', 'References'. If you can find a CV with these headings in (or create your own), delete the headings and put a line. Ask students to read the CV and guess what they think the missing headings were. Afterwards, they compare their ideas to the original. As well as helping to orientate students to the different parts of a CV, it's also a useful task on writing succinct sub-headings in business documentation.

8. Writing or recording a CV

Following on from activity 6, the next step is for students to write their own CVs. For an interesting variation, students could look at examples of video CVs which you will find online; this is where applicants supply a video of themselves talking about their background and experiences. Your students could create their own video CV using the cameras on their phones or a webcam and send it to you for feedback.

9. Interview questions

This activity is a way to review the grammar of question forms as well as generating interesting questions for a job interview role play. Write different types of question words on the board such as *What, Where, Why, How much, Which, Who, Can, Are, Is, Do, Does.* Put students into pairs and ask them to make a list of questions to ask in job interview situation using all the question words on the board; for example, *What are you currently doing? Where are you working? Why have you applied for this job? How much are you prepared to travel for this job? What is one of your main strengths and one weakness?* Once each pair of students have created a list, tell them to swap partners and take turns to role play a job interview situation with one of them asking their questions and the other person answering. To add authenticity to the role play, students could pretend that the interview is for the job they created in the advert in activity 5. As students interview, monitor their conversations and take notes for feedback afterwards.

10. Videoing job interviews

If you are helping students to prepare for job interviews, either by doing the type of role play outlined in 9, or perhaps for a real job that a student wants to apply for, try recording the job interviews in class on video. Afterwards, the student can watch their performance and you can also analyse the language they use and work on areas of weakness.

"When it comes to role playing a job interview, don't do anything too obscure or remote or complicated. Choose a job that the learners know and can relate to; for example applying for their own job (if in work), a job they had in the past, or (for pre-work learners) the 'job' of a brother, sister, parent, partner or best friend."

Keith Harding, author and trainer, London

10 activities for the topic of TECHNOLOGY and PRODUCTION

Technology is one of those topics which is continuously changing in the world of work and new words appear all the time; after all, a few years ago very few of us had heard terms like *app*, *social media*, *big data*, *analytics* and so on. Here's a selection of activities for lessons on this important business topic and they are all designed to be adapted to whatever type of technology the students might be interested in or have to use for their job.

1. Lead-in questions

Start off any lesson about technology by finding out how much your students use it. Ask questions such as: *What's your favourite piece of technology at home and at work? What technology can't you live without? Why not?*

2. Ranking technology

Choose a selection of modern technologies such as *computers, robots, jet aeroplanes, mobile phones, TVs, video conferencing equipment, bar codes* and write them around the board. Put students in pairs and ask them rank them in order of importance from the item of most importance to the item of least importance. Of course, their discussion will be highly subjective and they will have to support their views with reasons. Once the pairs have agreed, they can join another pair and present their lists. To extend the activity, the two pairs could try to agree on a final list through more discussion and compromise.

3. It's something which you use…

The following idea is a good guessing game which requires the students to use lots of descriptive language. Give the name of a different piece of technology to each student and write the phrase '*It's something you use for…*' on the board. Working in pairs, students have to take turns to define the technology for their partner who has to guess what the technology is. For example:

Student 1:   '*It's something you use for storing data.*'
Student 2:   '*Is it a server?*'
Student 1:   '*Not exactly, it's smaller.*'
Student 2:   '*Is it a portable hard drive?*'
Student 1:   '*No, even smaller.*'
Student 2:   '*A USB stick?*'
Student 1:   '*Correct*'.

Once they have defined their technology words, give them new ones or ask them to think of their own to define.

4. Sequence language

When explaining technology we often have to talk about different stages using sequencing language like *Firstly, Secondly, Thirdly, Next, Then, After that...* etc. To practise this language in a simple way you could give students a short set of instructions to follow. It could be a recipe to make a dish or part of an instruction manual to go with a commonly used piece of technology like a TV remote control. Students will have to read the instructions, then cover them, and try to summarise the sequence to a partner using the sequence words.

Unit 22

5. Mime the verb

To talk about using technology, students will often need verbs such as *turn up/down/on/off/round, push, press, switch on/off, close, open*, etc. These can often be taught through miming the action to the class and providing the word. Alternatively you might also be able to find a video which includes someone doing some of these actions (see next activity). Once you have taught the verbs, invite a student to the front of the class and whisper one of the verbs in their ear or show them the verb written on a piece of paper. They mime it to the class who have to guess the action. You can extend this activity if your students are all involved in similar jobs with technology (e.g. a class of engineers) and have each student come up and act one action they do in their job. The rest of the class has to guess and say which action from the job they are miming. It's a fun activity that can make the vocabulary memorable.

6. How to videos

Also on the theme of explaining how things work, there are literally thousands of online videos which people have made explaining how to do something or how some technical items work. Simply type in search terms such as '*How to change a tyre*' or '*How barcodes work*' and you'll find a video with someone presenting it. This kind of video can be a great source of listening practice and vocabulary to use with students in class.

7. Explain how it works

As a follow up to the previous activities in 3, 4 and 5 you could ask students to bring in an item of technology to class or a photograph of it. Ideally, it should be something that they use in their work. They have to prepare a short presentation explaining how it works. They could begin by making notes about how it works and you can walk around and help them with any vocabulary they need. Then students could present their technology to a partner, using sequence language in activity 4 and verbs from activity 5. When they are confident, they can present their explanation to the whole class. If your students enjoyed watching the 'How-to' videos mentioned in 6, they could even make their own video to put online!

8. Numbers and figures in technical documents

As well as speaking about technology, some of your students may have to work with technical documents in English. If they do, ask them to show you examples of the texts and try to incorporate parts of the text into your lessons (assuming the texts are relevant to the whole class). Many technical documents include lots of figures and numbers so a simple reading comprehension task is to write a selection of these around the board. Then give copies of the text to the students and ask them to try to find out what each figure or number refers to in the text. This develops their scanning skills when reading and it's very quick to prepare.

9. Technical documents with pictures

Technical documents and manuals – for example the type of documents you get with flat pack furniture or a new TV set – often include small images to go with each instruction. If you are working with this kind of text, then edit the document so that the images are separate from the text. Mix the images up and ask students to read the text. They have to number the images in the order they think they originally appeared in the document.

Unit 22

10. Write your own technical document

To bring together all the work that students may have done on technology and instructions, asking them at the end to write their own set of instructions can be very useful. They could write the instructions in pairs or groups. Here are two options for the type of instructions they might write:

▶ A set of instructions for a machine or piece of technology they regularly use.

▶ They could make up an imaginary piece of technology such as a robot to help them in their work. Then they write the instructions for using it – they can also add their own pictures if they like.

> "Don't be afraid to tell your students that you don't understand some technical content of a lesson; admitting ignorance is not a sign of weakness. Your expertise is in helping your learners communicate."
>
> **Lewis Lansford, Business English and Technical English trainer and writer, UK**

Unit 22

In a Business English teaching career you will come across many people from the world of Human Resources. You might well meet them directly as the people responsible for organising the training or you might have them as learners. They are usually good people to have in groups because they are used to dealing with people and are usually relaxed in a training environment.

1. Salary and benefits collocations

Although not necessarily responsible for actually organising the pay, which might be done by finance or payroll, the HR department is responsible for preparing information about working conditions, including salaries and benefits. You have to be careful discussing salaries in most Business English classrooms, but an activity based around packages is fine and usually leads to lively discussions. This task is deliberately active; just because you are teaching adults doesn't mean you can't get them up and moving. You will need a list of collocations connected to the theme such as:

- *company car*
- *private pension*
- *gym membership*
- *fringe benefits*
- *annual bonus*
- *subsidised canteen*
- *staff discount*
- *paid holiday*
- *annual medical*
- *health insurance*
- *language training*
- *clothing allowance*

Split the expressions into two parts and write them on pieces of paper (or use the photocopiable set of these words on p153). Stick all the words on the walls in different parts of the classroom. In pairs, the class have to move around the room, writing down full sentences with the words they find. When they have completed the list, check the sentences and correct collocations.

2. What motivates you most?

As a follow-on to the collocations in activity 1, ask students to work in pairs and rank the list of staff benefits in order of what motivates them most at work. At the end they compare their rankings with each other.

3. Defining six terms in a minute

Another extension to the list in activity 1 is to choose six of the collocations. Before the lesson, prepare a flipchart with the terms written on each page or, if you have a projector, they can be on separate slides. One student in turn sits in front of the flipchart or board so they cannot see the words but their colleagues can. The other students take it in turns to define the terms so that the person who cannot see them can guess them. For example:

Student A: Some staff get one of these so they can drive everywhere.

Student B: Company car!

Student A: Correct. This term means extra things you get in addition to your pay.

Ideally this activity is done against the clock. Can they define all six in a minute? A good stopwatch is available at http://www.online-stopwatch.com/countdown-timer/. The students gets 1 point for every word they guess correctly. Repeat the activity with a new set of words.

Unit 23

4. Redundancy role play

Tell the class that the board has decided to make one of the senior directors of a company redundant. Each group is responsible for representing one of the four or five directors. Choose from Managing Director, Sales Director, Marketing Director, Finance Director, Production Director and Research Director. In groups, build up a profile (professional and personal) of one candidate. You will want to know their age, experience, importance to the company, personal traits, etc. One student presents the profile to the rest of the class and pleads for them to be retained. The class then vote on who to make redundant.

5. Grievance role plays

While not making to want light of the problems certain people encounter at work, a grievance role play is a good way of practising the soft skills of active listening, being supportive and offering advice. Get the students to work in pairs initially. Put the following on strips of paper and distribute one to each A student. The B students are going to play the role of an HR manager listening to employees with problems.

1. *My colleague never finishes his work on time and the manager always asks me to help him. I have to finish my work alone and then someone else's. And he is paid more!*

2. *I have been late three times this month and my manager has sent me a warning letter. The problem is I have three children to get to school and no car to get here. The bus is often very slow.*

3. *I have a very noisy, messy colleague who sings to herself all day and eats sweets very loudly. Her desk is untidy and she must spend about an hour a day making tea. It's really annoying.*

4. *My manager never seems to have any ideas but every time we make a suggestion she puts it into action. She has just been promoted but we have been told there is no pay-rise this year.*

5. *I think my colleague's partner works for a competitor. She is really good at her job so it's a bit unfair to mention it.*

6. *I can't see why they picked him. She was so much better and so much nicer. I am not sure I want to stay if he is the new manager.*

(See p154 for a photocopiable set of these role plays.)

6. Introducing word building with 'manager'

Teaching students how to build words out of other words is very useful in Business English teaching. The word 'manager' is a good example because it can be turned into so many forms. For example: *manage* (verb) *manageable* (adjective) *manager* (noun/person), *management* (noun), *unmanageable* (with prefix). Show how these are built by writing them on the board. Then give students other words to build in a similar say such as *product, benefit, train, employ,* and *assist.* You could also use the photocopiable word-building table on p168.

7. The perfect manager

Brainstorm or supply 10 adjectives or phrases describing the perfect manager. Useful ones include:

▶ *A good listener*	▶ *Fair*	▶ *Able to delegate*	▶ *Organised*
▶ *Imaginative*	▶ *Charismatic*	▶ *Diplomatic*	▶ *Decisive*
▶ *Good with numbers*		▶ *A good communicator*	

Students work in pairs or groups and rank them from 1–10. Feed back as a class and collate the results. Managers in the class can see how well they measure up to the 'perfect' manager.

8. Training hours

An important aspect of HR is the whole area of training. An interesting activity is to set up a role play to discuss and prioritise training needs. Explain to the class that the company has a budget for up to 150 hours of training this year. The problem is how to decide how many hours should be allocated to each of the following training:

- ▶ English language training
- ▶ Presentation skills training
- ▶ Team building
- ▶ IT training
- ▶ Company policy training (compliance, internal procedures, appraisal system)
- ▶ Life skills training (art, cooking, yoga, etc.)
- ▶ Management training (motivation, assertiveness, time management, etc.)

You could also add other training options to the list if you think they might be relevant to some students. Put the students into small groups and set a time limit of 10 minutes to discuss how the hours will be allocated; for example, will they give 50 hours to English language training but only 20 hours to IT? Students should respond according to what they think the main needs are at their own company.

9. Balloon debate

This popular and classic debating game is unrealistic in terms of human resources but it does practise the language required for talking about people's strengths and arguing why some people should be let go. The aim is for the class to decide which person they want to keep alive during a balloon flight. The premise is that a group of people are in a hot air balloon which is losing height. Each person has to defend themselves before one is judged the loser and they have to jump. The process begins again until there is only one person left. You can use famous people who have done great things for the world like Tim Berners-Lee (inventor of the World Wide Web) or generic characters such as:

Head of a pharmaceutical company.	Swiss banker.
Nuclear scientist.	Nobel Peace Prize winner.
Developer of pesticide.	A paediatric surgeon.

Students work in groups of six or seven choosing one character each. The activity finishes when there is one person left. Give feedback on the language and arguments used.

10. Professional profile

An activity with a useful, authentic takeaway value is to look at professional, social networking profiles such as you find on sites like www.linkedin.com. It is perfectly usual these days to have your online profile and CV regularly updated. This does not suggest you are looking for a new job, but if something interesting comes along you may reconsider. Begin the class by looking at a selection of profiles. Some of your students might have theirs online, not necessarily in English. The point of a profile is to describe your skills, experience and strengths without being too wordy, egotistical or long. Have students work in pairs sketching out their profile and editing their partner's. They can then swap their profiles with other pairs who can add comments and suggestions. By the time each profile has been edited four or five times they should be ready to post. This sort of work can easily be posted on a class Facebook page or similar.

"On the topic of management, students like to hear from experts and they like what's current. The Harvard Business Review is a great source of fresh ideas."

Paul Dummett, Business English trainer and author

Business communication skills

Business communication skills are a key aspect of Business English and make it different from General English. Essentially, a 'communication skill' is the ability to put a message across in a particular form; for example, the skill could be presenting information, or participating effectively in a meeting. In business, people often take training courses in how to communicate more effectively in their own language. The course could include areas such as using body language positively, or how to negotiate with people from different cultures.

In the Business English classroom the teacher often has to help students with both the skill itself and also the language needed to carry it out in English. So you might find yourself introducing the language needed to structure a presentation and it could also be necessary to address a student's use of visual aids. Often, newer Business English teachers don't feel they are qualified to comment on non-linguistic areas of communication, but over time you will build your experience and potentially become quite an expert in how to train students to communicate effectively as well as speak English.

The section that follows looks at the whole area of developing students spoken communication skills. It begins by looking at business speaking in general and offers plenty of tips on ways to get students speaking and how to deal with errors and give feedback. The early units also look at ways of inputting and practising useful phrases for different communication skills including the use of frameworks.

The second half of the section looks directly at the key communication skills of social English and networking, meetings and discussions, telephoning, presenting and negotiating. You'll find a list of useful phrases to teach, tips on setting up and managing the classroom and practical ideas and activities to help develop your students' skills.

In your Business English teaching career one thing you will often hear is, 'I just want to talk' or 'I want to sound more English'. Speaking is the most stressful of the skills because you don't get much chance to prepare and your efforts are immediately open to the judgement of all the people present as you open your mouth. It is very tempting to just let your learners chat away, correcting them occasionally and taking notes to look at later. Unfortunately, this approach will not always work and is a bit of a waste given the wide range of possibilities to get your learners practising speaking in a more systematic way.

1. Discussion questions

Probably the simplest way to lead into any lesson or topic is to write three or four discussion questions on the board. Remember that to make these generative you need to use open question words (what, where, why, how, etc.) as opposed to closed questions (are you, do you, does it… etc.). For example, a question like 'What do you think makes a bad manager?' will generate more discussion than 'Are you a manager?'

2. Controlled dialogues

When introducing situational or functional language which you want students to use, a controlled dialogue is a good starting point. Present the situation either by explaining it or maybe showing a picture of two people talking. Elicit from the class what the first person might be saying and write it on the board. Then elicit the next sentence and so on until you have around 10 lines of conversation on the board. Students work in pairs and try reading it together. Once they have read it a few times, delete some of the lines from the board so that they have to say the dialogue again but this time try to remember certain missing lines. You can continue like this until the whole dialogue disappears and students can repeat it from memory.

3. Drilling

As part of activities such as dialogue building in activity 2, drilling is a key part of helping students to improve their speaking. The chance for students to listen to you say a sentence and then for them to repeat it shouldn't take more than a three or four seconds. Some teachers worry that drilling might be boring for students but as long as it's done quickly and with pace, your students will always appreciate the chance to listen to and repeat a sentence so they feel confident saying it in a freer situation later on.

4. Mini-presentations

Mini-presentations and talks are often mentioned in this book because they are such good and authentic practice and offer you real snapshots of your students' abilities. Whether prepared or spontaneous, timed or not, with slides or without, making a presentation is a useful activity. Explaining why things happen, reporting back on an event, making suggestions for solving a particular problem or simply making an observation are all interesting topics for students to talk about.

Unit 24

5. Talking about images

Although usually associated with exam preparation classes, talking about an image is a very useful activity which allows you to feed in new vocabulary either during or after the commentary. Images showing processes, facilities or equipment are really helpful and can be found through Google Images or YouTube. A paused video clip is just as useful as a still image.

6. Role plays

There are various theories that playing a role allows you to speak in a different and possibly more confident way than when you speak as yourself. Be that as it may, Business English has numerous opportunities to play roles, either in simple situational dialogues or in more complex communicative activities such as meetings. Playing a role allows the learner to really focus on how they are speaking rather than what they are saying. For a learner, one of the most difficult aspects of learning is to have the ideas and express them simultaneously so at various stages of the course it is useful to supply them with the ideas.

7. Small talk

At the start and end of any lesson a teacher will want to make small talk with students with questions like, 'So, how was your weekend?' or 'Have you had a busy day?' Students enjoy this stage of the lesson because it helps them achieve one of their main aims, to be more at ease and relaxed in English. Since it is such an important part of their learning be careful not to stifle any attempts by them to initiate conversation, indeed encourage it as much as possible.

8. Games

Any sort of word game is useful speaking practice and every teacher has their own personal favourite often based on parlour games or quiz shows from TV or radio. You'll also see a photocopiable example of a board game on p159 which can be adapted to target different language areas. As a teacher you need to bear in mind how long games should last, how competitive they should be and most of all make sure that the class understands the pedagogic value of them. Note that some students might not perceive classroom 'games' as real learning so you may have to convince them slowly of the value by limiting how much you use them at first.

9. Story telling

Everybody tells stories, it is one of the great human activities, reporting back on events, trips, incidents, etc. As adults we are desperate to be able to do this in the language we are learning. Encourage this right from the start and allocate time into the course for students to tell a story. It can be something which happened, something invented, something funny, it doesn't matter. The main thing is to give them the opportunity to do the kind of thing they do in their own language in English.

10. Simulations/case studies

Most course books have activities where students have to take part in a meeting to share ideas and opinions about a particular issue. There is usually a substantial amount of reading and audio/video to study first of all so that everyone has access to information which will help them shape their views. One disadvantage to the case study is that the reading/listening phase can sometimes take substantially more time than the speaking. Popular on MBA and other management courses, they can be very successful on Business English courses but you need to know which ones work and which ones need simplifying. Standard examples include choosing the best recruit for a position, deciding on a relocation or outsourcing strategy and developing a greenfield site.

"If your learners have access to the internet outside of class, try setting oral/aural homework tasks that practise listening and speaking skills. Use websites such as Voxopop to set a question, which students listen to and then record their reply. Students invariably like to submit a good answer, so they will usually practise several times in order to get it right."

Angela Buckingham, ELT writer and teacher trainer, UK

Unit 24

10 considerations about teaching communication skills

Business communication skills include giving presentations, networking and socialising, attending and running meetings, and negotiating. Most business people will have already attended training sessions focusing on these skills in their own language. Inevitably, students of Business English are interested in learning the language they will need to give a presentation or chair a meeting in English. Here are 10 points worth considering when planning to incorporate communication skills training in your lessons.

1. Identify the language

Communication skills require certain high frequency vocabulary and expressions. The vocabulary will relate to the content of what is being discussed (e.g. a meeting about finance) and the expressions that will help to structure the event (e.g. the expressions needed to run a meeting such as 'Let's start our meeting', 'Can you speak first?').

2. The non-linguistic features of skill

As well as spoken language, a communication skill includes non-linguistic features including eye contact, gesture, body language, visual aids, appearance, rapport and delivery. So knowing the language alone is not enough to be effective in the skill. How much you deal with these formally in class will depend on the type of students you are working with. (See next tip.)

3. The language/skill balance

How much you actually 'teach' the language or the 'skill' will depend on your student's level of experience. Clearly, if you have a student with lots of experience in presenting or networking, then you probably won't give too much advice on this area; in fact you could ask the student to comment on what makes a good presentation or how a meeting can be more effective. But if you are teaching students with little or no experience of the working world, then they will rely on you to provide formal training on being effective in the skill.

4. Feedback

In English classes we are used to giving feedback on language but with communications skills the teacher will also need to be prepared to give feedback on the skill itself. So you might comment on the student's body language or the structure of a presentation. (See Unit 36.)

5. Cultural awareness

Our students' cultural background will affect how they communicate, even if they are using English as the lingua franca. For example, in a social situation one student might think it's appropriate to chat about their family life whereas for the other person it's considered better to avoid this topic and talk about working life. As well as the actual content of the discussion, culture also affects how people react; for example, in a negotiation one person from North America might assume that any statement requires an immediate response whereas someone from parts of Asia might consider that a respectful pause after the other person has spoken is the polite thing to do. This kind of cultural difference can in fact affect a communication situation so it's useful to be aware of it and even raise it as a point of discussion in your lessons.

6. Opportunities to practise

Any lesson with the aim of helping students to improve their communication skills must involve lots of opportunity to practise. If students need to prepare a presentation in English for work, then include lots of time in the lesson for them to try it out, to receive feedback (from you or from their peers), and then to do it again. For developing areas such as telephoning skills, you might want to set up role play situations so students have to place themselves in a situation where, for example, they have to deal with an angry customer on the other end of the phone.

7. Recording the communication

Recording the students giving a presentation or talking on the phone is a very useful way for them to self-assess their work and to try again. So you might record an audio version only or you could video the students. This is especially useful if you want them to think about the kind of message they are giving through their body language, for example.

8. Analyse their skills

Communicating well in a foreign language requires a lot of practise and a high level of self-awareness. Your learners will need to analyse their performance individually and via peer feedback in order to become aware of where they need to make progress. They might have issues of intonation or speed of delivery, recurring grammar mistakes or posture and eye contact issues which impact on their ability to communicate. Not everything can be improved at once so they need to prioritise areas to work on.

9. Use and learn from what they do in L1

Usually a learner is trying to transfer a skill they have already developed in their mother tongue. There might be cultural aspects which influence the same skill carried out in English, but more often than not they can use what they know to perform in English. What they need to avoid is translating everything directly from L1. Rhetorical styles, sentence length and interactive patterns do vary from culture to culture but there is still a lot which can be transferred. Someone who has chaired a meeting in their own language will be more able to do it in English than someone who hasn't.

10. Discuss the theory

Communications skills is sufficiently developed as a subject that you can, if your students want to, discuss the theory. Whether you are trying to get them to write more engaging emails, negotiate more confidently or simply handle a conversation before a meeting, there are theories and tips which are worth discussing. The internet is full of advice for succeeding at work and these websites are a rich source of resources for discussion. Many adult learners are reluctant to change unless they know why, so these resources also help motivate them.

10 ways to use frameworks

Frameworks are a popular tool in Business English teaching. As the name suggests, they provide a 'framework' for structuring the spoken or written language you want students to use. Often, they are presented as diagrams or flowcharts but they can also simply take the form of bullet-point lists which guide the students. The language used in a framework might be a single word or heading to prompt the student. Alternatively, it might contain an expression or phrase which you want the student to use. Here are some examples of frameworks aimed at different business language areas and suggestions on ways to vary them for your own context.

1. Structure

This framework shows the structure of standard presentation. Students can refer to it when preparing their own presentations.

2. Language input

Another use for a framework like the one above is to put it on the board and list a variety of expressions. Students have to categorise the expressions in the relevant parts of the framework. So, in the example above, you might list presentation language such as *Good morning everyone, moving onto my next point, referring back to my second point, any questions?* Students match the expressions to one or more of the five stages and then they can use the expressions appropriately in their own presentations.

3. Dialogues

The framework below is designed for students working in pairs and practising a controlled telephone role play situation. So Student A follows the prompts on the left and Student B, the prompts on the right. As with activity 1, this framework uses prompts so that students have to follow the instructions in each speech bubble, however the teacher could replace these with expressions to use such as *'Hello,...speaking. Can I help you?', 'Could I speak to...?', 'I'm sorry he's ...', 'Can I leave a message?'*

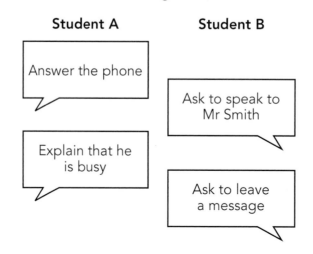

4. Mixed ability frameworks

Frameworks like the one shown in activity 3 can also work well with mixed ability classes. You could redesign the telephoning framework above so that Student A has the same prompts in his/her squares on the left-hand side but Student B has nothing written in the squares on the right-hand side. Clearly, the challenge is greater for Student B and so you would assign this role to a student with a higher level of English.

5. Three-way discussion

The example below is from a lesson giving practice in having a meeting. The teacher has introduced some basic language for expressing opinions, agreeing and disagreeing and now students work in groups of three (A, B or C). The teacher suggests a simple topic for them to discuss and then, as in activity 3, they create the conversation by following the prompts. Unlike 3, the structure of a discussion like this is more complex, so the final box is a '?' indicating that at this stage Student C can respond in any way he/she wants to and the three students can continue the discussion freely. It's a useful way of taking students from controlled practice into freer practice.

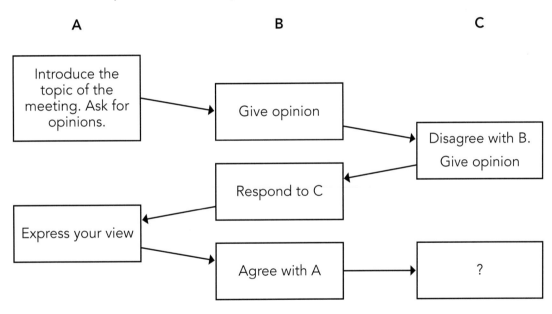

6. Describing a process

This framework is useful when working with students who need to explain processes in their job. Unlike the previous frameworks, the teacher has put some language in each box that he/she wants the student to say. Then the student needs to make notes about each step in the process including any key vocabulary. It's a useful tool for preparing the explanation and makes sure students use certain language. A similar framework would also work well with the language of cause and effect (e.g. *because of, due to, leads to*, etc). A photocopiable handout of the following process diagram can be found on p156.

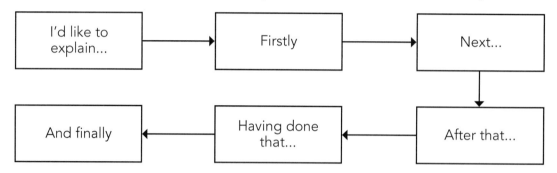

7. Bullet point lists

Frameworks don't have to include the visual element of the diagram. A simple framework can take the form of a list written on the board which students follow step by step. Here's an example of one written to help students structure the paragraphs in an application for a job:

▶ Explain why you are writing and where you saw the advert.

▶ Give some basic background and refer to your attached CV.

▶ Outline your availability for an interview.

▶ End formally.

8. Ordering the framework

As a variation to the approach in activity 7, you can also present a framework list with the items in the incorrect order. Students have to number the stages correctly before then trying to follow the steps. In the example below, the teacher has been teaching the language for negotiating and then puts the stages of a negotiation on the board. The students must reorder them correctly:

▶ Discuss the conditions.

▶ Introduce the initial offer.

▶ Reject the initial offer.

▶ Find out what the other person would accept.

▶ Make a new offer.

▶ Accept the new offer with conditions.

▶ Make a final deal.

▶ Explain what might be possible.

Once the students have reordered the steps, they can go ahead and role play a negotiation.

(Answer to above: *Introduce the initial offer, Reject the initial offer, Find out what the other person would accept, Explain what might be possible, Make a new offer, Accept the new offer with conditions, Discuss the conditions, Make a final deal.*)

9. Repurposing diagrams

If you are working in a company, you might have access to different type of diagrams and flowcharts designed to illustrate aspects of the company's business. These can often be converted into framework-type activities. For example, if you have diagram showing the management structure of a company, it could form the basis of students' presentations about the company. Or a flowchart showing the process of customer care at the company would provide good practice with the sequencing language shown in activity 6.

10. Tailor-made frameworks

Once your students have become familiar with you providing frameworks and how they can be used in class, you can ask them to create their own, based on the needs of their job. So if they make certain types of phone-calls, they could try to illustrate the structure of such calls using a similar framework to the one shown in activity 3. In one-to-one lessons, creating a new framework can even form part of the actual lesson with the teacher and student discussing the different stages of, for example, a process relevant to the student's work.

"I like using lists in the classroom. So sometimes I ask my students to think of a process in their job or in their company and list all the stages in that process. Then they present the list to the class. If your students do the same job, they can compare their lists and see if they agree."

Lindsay Clandfield, teacher, trainer, author

Read more about how Lindsay uses lists with students in his blog posts at www.myetpedia.com.

10 tips on correcting errors and giving feedback

Unit 27

When students work on their speaking and oral communication skills such as presenting, socialising and meetings they will expect and want feedback. There are a number of considerations when correcting and different ways to approach correction.

1. Correcting language

When deciding to correct a language error, you'll need to think whether you correct everything or just the mistakes that affect the effectiveness of the communication.

2. Correcting non-linguistic aspects

When you give feedback in general on the communication, your decision will be whether to comment on the use of skills such as body language, use of slides, how well the student chaired a meeting and so on; in other words, it will depend on whether you see your role as commenting on the non-linguistic aspects of the communication as well as the language used.

3. Instant error correction

Sometimes while students are speaking you might hear them make a mistake and feel you need to correct them straight away. This might be appropriate if the students are working in pairs and you won't disrupt their speaking too much by interrupting.

4. Delayed error correction

Unlike in tip 3, if a group of students are running a meeting or one student is giving a presentation to the whole class, then it won't be appropriate to interrupt and correct the mistake. In this case, it's preferable to listen and make a note of any mistakes on a piece of paper. It is also useful to highlight some good language as part of this feedback.

5. Whole class feedback

If you noted down any errors or feedback points while groups of students were talking, then set aside 10 minutes (or longer if necessary) at the end of the lesson and feedback on common mistakes they made.

6. Personalised feedback

Obviously in a one-to-one class it's much easier to give personalised feedback to the student than it is to a number of students. However, if you do have a group of students speaking you can make notes on errors made by particular students and then write their particular errors on a sheet of paper. Afterwards, each student receives their mistakes and you ask them to study and correct the sentences for homework.

7. Record and correct

Listening for errors and suggesting ways to improve a performance can sometimes be difficult to do in real time. So using a video camera or recording equipment is one option because you can listen to the students afterwards and note down their difficulties. In a one-to-one class you can even integrate this into the lesson by recording the student and then playing it back so that you and the student work together to pick out any problems with what they said. Video recording works especially well if students are giving presentations.

8. Self correction

If you like the idea of recording your students (see 7), then you can also ask students to record themselves and listen in order to self-correct. Many students can benefit from this technique because they are able to spot their own errors when they listen back to what they said. You will still need to add your own feedback, but developing the skill of self-correction is giving the students a long-term study strategy.

9. Peer correction

Peer correction is asking students to give each other feedback. For example, one student might give a presentation and another student (or group of students) gives feedback afterwards. This approach needs to be handled sensitively. The students need to trust each other and feel that comments from their peers will be useful.

10. Feedback forms

If you use an approach such as 'peer feedback' (see tip 9), the students giving the feedback will also need some guidance on what to give feedback on. So it's always helpful if they have a feedback form designed for the task (see p163) which they complete and then use as the basis for their spoken feedback afterwards. One final point to note is that business students may be qualified to comment on the communication skill itself and say, for example, if the speaker's message was clear or if they used visuals effectively. However, they are not language experts so you will still need to give feedback on the language and any errors.

"If students are doing a speaking fluency activity, note down some of the errors. You could write them on the board, disguising the content perhaps so that others don't know who made the mistake. Give students five minutes to work in pairs and 'spot the mistake'."

Rachel Appleby, trainer and author, Budapest

10 ways to introduce and practise useful phrases

When teaching business communication skills, we often introduce students to sets of useful phrases. You can look at different sets of phrases in Unit 29 (Social English), Unit 31 (Meetings and discussions), Unit 33 (Telephoning) and Unit 38 (Negotiating). There are different ways to introduce these kinds of expressions and then to practise them in a controlled way before giving students freer practice. Here are 10 ways to introduce and practise any kinds of phrases that you might teach students for different skills and business situations.

1. A script

Choose a set of phrases and write a script between some business people in which they use the phrases. For example, a simple script to introduce the phrases in Unit 29 (Social English) might start like this:

Jurgen: Hi. My name's Jurgen Vettorel. Nice to meet you.

Lucia: Nice to meet you too. I'm Lucia Marks. I'm with OIG. Who do you work for?

Jurgen: I'm a consultant so I'm freelance.

Lucia: That's interesting.

Once you've written your script, you could put students into pairs and give each a pair a copy to read aloud (or put the script on the board). Students could underline useful phrases in the script or rewrite it to suit their own context.

2. Recordings

As the phrases are all spoken, it's useful for students to hear them in context. You could get colleagues to read your script in activity 1 aloud and then record it. Play the recording back in class and students note down which phrases are useful. You'll also find that many Business English materials include professionally made recordings which provide model dialogues.

3. Listen and fill in the gaps

Another useful technique to focus on the phrases is to listen to a recording of the script and then give students a copy of the script with certain words or the whole phrase missing and the students have to fill in as they listen. So the script in activity 1 it might look like this:

Jurgen: Hi. My name's Jurgen Vettorel. 1_____ to meet you.

Lucia: Nice to meet you 2_____. I'm Lucia Marks. I'm with OIG. 3_____ do you work for?

Jurgen: I'm a consultant so I'm freelance.

Lucia: That's 4_____.

4. Listen and tick

Give students a copy of a set of phrases. They listen to the scripted recording and tick the phrases they hear. Alternatively, you could read a script aloud, especially if it's for a presentation. For example, a teacher could start reading a presentation aloud like this: 'Good morning everyone and thank you for coming. Today, I'm going to be talking about developments in retail websites. I'd like to begin with showing you some examples, then we'll look at my top 10 rules for web design. Feel free to ask questions during my talk…' While listening, students tick the phrases in Unit 29 or use the photocopiable page on p158.

5. Cut up script

Make copies of a script and cut it up line by line. Give a cut up version of the script to pairs or groups of three. They read the lines and try to put the script back together in the correct order. This is a useful way to focus on how the different phrases relate to each other. You can use the photocopiable example on page 157.

6. Hum the missing word

Many phrases used in Business English are fixed expressions; this means that words within the expression follow a pattern. So the final word in a phrase like 'Nice to meet you too' cannot change to 'Nice to meet you also.' That would be wrong. One way to provide simple practice with learning these fixed expressions is to read the phrase but miss out a word and 'hum' instead. Students have to listen and guess the missing word. Here are some examples from the phrases in Unit 35. The teacher has taken phrases for giving presentations and makes a humming noise where the word is in square brackets.

Thank [you] for inviting me.

The title of my [presentation] is Human Resources in the twenty-first century.

I'll be happy to take questions at the [end].

That [brings] me to my next point.

Take a [look] at this graph.

Let me explain in more [detail].

That's a [good] question.

I'm sorry, I don't think I quite [follow].

That's all we have [time] for.

It can be a fun activity and students can get competitive when trying to call out the missing word. For a quieter version, students could write down what they think the missing word is and you can check their answers at the end. Alternatively, put students in pairs, and they take turns to read out phrases in the same way to their partner who must guess what word is missing where he/she hears a hum.

7. Eliciting phrases by their function

You can start introducing functional phrases by eliciting suggestions from the students. Begin by writing functional headings on the board, like these which are for the language of meetings and discussions:

Interrupting	*Stating the aims*	*Asking for opinions*
Preventing an interruption	*Giving an opinion*	*Partially agreeing*
Summing up	*Checking understanding*	
Disagreeing	*Agreeing*	

Put students in pairs or small groups and ask them to think of one phrase for each heading. For example, interrupting – *"Sorry, can I interrupt you for a moment?"* If students have problems thinking of phrases, ask them to translate phrases they use in their own language. As they come up with ideas for phrases, check the language is both correct and sounds natural. Finally, ask students to share their ideas for phrases with other pairs and write their ideas on the board under each of the headings. By the end, you should have built up a collection of useful phrases for the whole class to look at. You could then make copies of the list of phrases in Unit 31 to give to each students to compare with their ideas. They can add any of their own new phrases to the list.

8. Cut-up phrases

Having phrases on separate pieces of paper is time-consuming because you'll need to spend time cutting up a number of sets for a class. However, once it's done, they become a very useful tool. As an example of how cut-up phrases might be used, here is an activity that follows on from the previous activity in 7.

Make copies of the phrases for the language of meetings on p161 in the photocopiable section of this book. Cut up the phrases and give out one set to groups of three or four students. Write the 10 functional headings on the board again as in activity 7. Tell each group to categorise the cut up phrases according to the headings. By the end, each group should have 10 small piles of phrases categorised by functional heading on the desk in front of them. They can check with other groups to see if they agree.

9. Deal the phrases

As a follow-up to the idea of using cut-up phrases in activity 8, the groups can deal out the phrases for the language of meetings and discussions to each other so everyone has an equal number of phrases. Explain that the group is going to have a simple meeting to discuss a topic such as 'How can we make the offices more environmentally friendly?' You could choose a discussion topic related to anything you have been doing in class recently but choose something that doesn't require too much subject knowledge, as the main purpose of this exercise is to practise the phrases. Explain that one student goes first and starts the meeting using a suitable phrase in their hand. As they use the phrase, they lay it in the middle of the table. Then the player on their left must try to continue the meeting by using another of the phrases in their hand. Now the next player on the left has a turn so that the discussion continues to flow in a circle round the group. Every time the next speaker must use one phrase in their hand correctly. As the game progresses, speakers will start to run out of suitable phrases; if they can't use a phrase in their hand they must miss a go and it passes to the next player. The winner is the person who uses all the phrases first.

10. Tick the phrases you use

Once students become familiar with different phrases to use in different situations, it's always helpful if they keep a copy of the phrases with them for reference. For example, you could give students copies of the phrases listed in units 29, 31, 33 or 38. Many students will find it useful to keep these copies on their desks at work but you can also make use of them in class. For example, when you set up a role play, or simulate a group meeting, students could tick the phrases they use during the speaking practice. You could make the rule that they can only use a phrase once so that next time they have to find a different way of saying the same thing.

You might come across students who say to you, 'I don't need English for my job. I already know how to talk about that. I need help with making conversation and talking about general topics in English'. So what these students probably want is 'Social English' or English for small talk, which is as much a part (if not more so) of doing business in English as is any specialist area such as finance, sales or logistics.

Find out from the students the types of situations they are in when making small talk. Some might attend conferences and have to strike up conversations with people they don't know. Others might take a lot of telephone calls which can also involve elements of small talk. To start students off, you could present them with these 10 sets of useful expressions for starting and maintaining conversations in social situations.

1. Introducing yourself

Hello, my name's …

Pleased/Nice to meet you.

Nice to meet you too.

I'm in charge of/responsible for…

2. Finding out about the other person

Who do you work for? / Who are you with?

What do you do?

Where are you from?

How long have you been with …? / How long have you worked at/for…?

Do you know …?

3. Building on general topics

So have you been with [your company] a long time?

When did you start?

Who were you with before that? / Who did you work for before that?

Have you always lived in …?

Tell me more about …

What's it like?

4. Making connections

A lot of small talk involves trying to find out things you have in common with the other person.

I used to work with someone called [name]. Do you know him/her?

Have you ever worked for …?

Do you have any children? (not appropriate in all cultures but it can be very generative in the correct context)

I studied … at university. What about you?

Do you play much golf/tennis/sport?

5. Showing interest in what the other person says

Sometimes teachers feel that teaching this kind of language is strange and can sound insincere. In fact, we use this kind of technique to show interest all the time so it's a useful type of language.

That's interesting.

Really?

I see.

I didn't know that.

Great!

6. Conversation starters at an event

Many business people have to start conversations with people they have never met before at events such as conferences, trade fairs, training events and so on. This can require some kind of phrase to break the ice with someone who is next to you.

Is this seat free?

How are you finding the [conference]?

Have you attended many good talks today?

Is it your first time here?

Have you had far to come today?

7. Offering, accepting, declining

Would you like a …?

Can I get you a drink?

Thanks, I'd like a …

That's very kind of you. I'll have a …

No thanks, I'm OK.

8. Introducing others

Let me introduce you to …

Have you met …?

Do you know …?

This is …. She's in charge of …

9. Keeping in touch

Here's my card.

Do you have a card?

What's your number?

Keep in touch.

Give me a call next time you're in [New York].

Unit 29

10. Saying goodbye

I'm afraid I have to go.
It was really nice meeting/talking to you.
Maybe I'll see you again soon.
I look forward to seeing you again.
Goodbye/Bye.

"People like to do business with people they like. Obviously we can't teach our students to be nice people, but we can make sure they are equipped with the language they need to ensure they come across as a nice, decent sort of person that we'd all want to do business with. Social English is basically about impression management."

Vicki Hollett, Business English trainer, author and creator of www.simpleenglishvideos.com

10 fluency activities for Social English

The types of phrases students might need for socialising and networking are in Unit 29. Once you've presented them, you'll need to provide lots of opportunity to practise this language and develop students' confidence with speaking in social situations. Here are 10 activities for practising the language of Social English, developing fluency and the skill of networking. The first four activities focus on question forms, which students need to practise to show interest in the other speaker(s). Activities 5, 6 and 7 offer the chance to talk about different topics and use a range of vocabulary as well consider the skills needed to build conversations. Activity 8 is a way to make sure students use expressions taught in your lessons and the final two activities use business cards as the basis for free practice.

1. First day small talk

This simple activity is for the first day with a new class and practises basic question forms for making conversation with a new person. Invite students to ask you questions and write them on the board, e.g. *Where are you from? How long have you worked as a …?* Write around 10 on the board and then answer them. Next, put students in pairs and ask them to take turns asking and answering the questions on the board so they find out about each other.

2. Guess the question

Another activity that is useful for students to get to know each other and also practise the language for making conversations is to ask students to think of five important facts about their life and to write down one word associated with each. So if it's the city they are from, they can write it down. The word can also be something less obvious like the number of years they have worked for their current company (so they might write a number such as '10' meaning 10 years). Next, put the students in pairs. The students show each other their list of five words and take turns to guess the question the word will answer; for example, *Where are you from?* or *How long have you worked for your current company?* The winner is the student who guesses the questions for all five words.

3. Dice questions

The aim of this activity is to practise question forms to make small talk about different topics. You will need some dice. Students work in pairs and with two dice per pair. Write the following dice numbers (1-6) on the board:

Topics: 1 = sports and hobbies, 2= travel and holidays, 3 = work, 4 = news and media, 5 = family and friends, 6 = weather

Questions: 1 = what, 2 = where, 3 = how, 4 = when, 5 = which, 6 = why

Students take turns to roll the two dice. One dice is for topics so if it lands on 4, the students must create a question about 'news and media'. The other dice indicates the question word they must use, so if it lands on 5, they must start their question with 'Which'. So the student who rolled can ask a question such as 'Which newspaper do you normally read?' and the other student must answer. It requires quick-thinking and generates a whole range of question types.

4. Developing open questions

Effective conversationalists tend to build small talk by asking a closed question (one that can be answered with a simple 'yes' or 'no') followed by an open question starting with *what, why, how, where* etc. For example:

A: Is this your first time at this conference?

B: Yes, it is.

A: How are you finding it?

B: Great, thanks. It's been really interesting so far.

Students can develop this skill with the following activity which is also a useful way to practise and revise the language of question forms. Write a list of general Yes/No questions on the board such as:

1. Do you play much sport?

2. Do you like Italian food?

3. Are you from Sweden?

4. Do you often travel for your job?

5. Is this your first time at this conference?

Next, put students into A/B pairs. A begins by asking B one of the *Yes/No* questions on the board and B replies with a *Yes/No* answer. Then A must create a follow-up question which is open and B must reply. Then they switch roles and repeat the activity with a different question. Continue until they have used all the questions on the board.

5. One-minute topics

A simple fluency warmer for a lesson is to have a box full of pieces of paper with different topics to talk about. These could include general topic headings such as 'sport' or 'films' or more specific headings such as 'your favourite day of the year' or 'the least interesting aspect of your job'. Students work in pairs and take turns to pick a piece of paper out of the box. They have one minute to talk about the topic while their partner times them. If they manage to speak non-stop for a minute they get a point. Then they swap roles and the other student has a go. You can update the topics in the box from time-to-time with new topics; in fact, if you choose topic areas recently covered in class then it's a good way to revise recently taught language.

6. Common topics

Many business networking conversations centre around finding things you have common with the other person. To practise this skill and the language required, put students into groups of four or five. Write a selection of small talk topics randomly on the board such *sport, family, travel, food, politics, films, music, money, holidays, pets, weather*. Next, explain that they are at a networking event and they have five minutes to make conversation about any of the topics on the board. The aim is to find as many commonalities as possible with the other people in the group. For example, a conversation might go like this:

A: Have any of you ever visited New York?

B: No, I haven't.

C: Yes, I went there last year.

A: Really? I was there last year as well…

Every time a student finds something they have in common with another person in the group they give themselves a point. So for the conversation above, A and C both get a point for having both been to New York whereas B does not. The strategy to gaining the most points in this activity is to introduce as many varied topics as possible to try and find commonalities with other people in the group. The competitive element mixed with fun and rivalry makes it great fluency practice and really helps to develop networking skills. (This activity is based on idea from Daniel Pink's excellent book *To sell is human*, published by Canongate, 2012.)

7. Taboo topics

This is a variation on the previous activity which focuses students' attention on cultural differences and strategies for avoiding talking about certain topics. As with the previous activity, students work in small groups and you need to write a variety of topics for small talk on the board like this: *sport, family, religion, travel, food, politics, films, music, salaries, holidays, pets, weather.*

Explain to the students that in certain cultures it isn't appropriate to discuss certain topics; for example, some cultures will not talk about topics such as salaries or religion. Tell each student to choose two topics off the board which they will not talk about. These don't have to be real cultural choices, but random such as 'films' and 'weather'.

Next, tell students that they have five minutes to make small talk with each other about the topics on the board. In that time, each student must try to work out which two topics are taboo for each of the speakers. This requires students to try and introduce each of the topics into the conversation in order to establish which students are avoiding them. At the end of the five minutes, the students tell each other which topics they think each other chose.

It's a fun activity that raises their awareness of how culture can affect conversation and also practises a range of social English skills.

8. Tick the expression

If you have recently taught phrases (see Unit 29) to students for Social English such as *'Have we met before?'* or *'Do you have much free time for sport?'*, then provide a list to give to students. Then put them in pairs or small groups of three and set a time limit of two or three minutes in which they must make conversation and try to use as many of the phrases as possible in an appropriate way. When they use a phrase they tick it on their list. At the end of the time limit, students count the number of expressions they ticked and see which person in the group used the most.

Unit 30

9. Business cards

Business cards are really useful in the classroom; collect them from anyone (e.g. from past students) and keep them safe. Whenever you set up a role play in class or try out some of the activities above, you can add variety by giving a business card to a student and saying *'You are this person'*. It's an opportunity for a student to play the part of someone else and imagine the type of topics and language that person might use. It also adds variety to any task and an element of fun which role play can bring. One simple low-level activity to practise basic question forms is to put students in pairs and give each students a different business card. Students must start a conversation in which they ask and answer questions about the details of the other person.

10. Social English board game

Board games can be used for a whole range of activity types and work especially well for practising language in social situations. Make one copy of the photocopiable board on p159 for pairs of students or groups of three. They will need a dice and each need a counter (a coin, for example) and place it on the START square. They take turns to roll the dice and move their counter round the board. As they land on each square, they follow the instructions and practise speaking in a range of social situations.

"Mix your class around, so that students become accustomed to listening to as wide a variety of speakers as possible."

Angela Buckingham, ELT writer and teacher trainer, UK

10 sets of useful phrases for meetings and discussions

Most of your students will attend meetings of some kind. Some might be quite formal with a chair, an agenda and minutes taken, whereas others will be more informal discussions. However, in all meetings and discussion there are some stages and expressions which are fairly generic so it's worth teaching them to most of your students. Here are 10 sets of phrases normally taught in a lesson on the language of meetings and discussions.

1. Stating the aims of the meeting

The purpose of the meeting is to …
The aim of this discussion is to …
What we want to do by the end of this meeting is to …

2. Asking for opinions

What do you think about …?
What's your opinion?
Do you agree with/about …?

3. Giving an opinion

I think …
In my opinion …
It's my view that …

4. Agreeing

I agree.
You're absolutely right.
I think so too.

5. Disagreeing

I disagree.
I don't agree.
I can't agree with you.

6. Partially agreeing

I agree with you up to a point but …
A lot of what you are saying is true but …
Yes, but …

7. Interrupting

Can I interrupt you there because …?
Before you continue I'd like to say that …
I'd like to say something …
But …

8. Preventing an interruption

Please, let me finish ...
Sorry, but I'd like to finish ...
Just one more thing and then you can speak ...

9. Checking understanding

So what you're saying is ...?
Let me check I've understood you ...
So if I've understood you correctly ...

10. Summing up the discussion

So let's sum up what we've discussed so far.
Can I just summarise what we've agreed?
We've agreed/decided that ...

"In lessons on the language of meetings, I find that brainstorming the expressions students use in meetings in their own mother tongue is a useful way to recognise the importance of the equivalent expressions in English."

Penny McLarty, Business English teacher, Oxford, UK

10 instant mini-meetings

To practise the language of meetings and discussions (see Unit 31) you will need to set up mini-meetings with students working in small groups of between three and five. It's always helpful to have one student as the group leader or chair to start the meeting off (and possibly control it). As students become more competent with the language of meetings you can start to make your meeting simulations more and more complex. Note that the extended case studies and scenarios that often appear in Business English coursebooks are excellent for this. However, if your aim is simply to get students to work with certain language and phrases, then try to keep the topics of your meetings simple so that not too much specific detail is required and students can add their own ideas.

Below are 10 ideas for mini-meetings. Choose one and write it on the board so that students can discuss it. Tell one student to make notes during the meeting so that each group can present their decisions to the rest of the class at the end of the meeting. As you listen to the different meetings, take notes on the language you hear and give feedback afterwards.

1. A local tour

Plan and organise a one-day tour of your local area for a group of five VIPs. The visitors are all different ages and genders.

2. Choose a charity

Your company collects money every year for charity. This year it has raised $3,500. List five possible charities it could give the donation to and say why. Then decide which deserves to receive the money.

3. Celebrity endorsement

You are planning a new marketing campaign. List the names of five different famous people who could represent your brand. Then select the best one.

4. The time capsule

You company is building a new headquarters. It has decided to put a time capsule in the foundations. Brainstorm 10 items to include which will tell people in the future about your company.

5. Employee of the month

Your company would like to introduce a new 'employee of the month' award. Brainstorm a list of criteria for the award so you can decide which employee receives it.

6. Team-building day

Your company is merging with another and employees from the two sites are going to start working together in the same building. Organise and timetable a day of 'getting to know each other' activities and team-building events.

7. Family fun day

Plan a family fun day for employees and their families. Discuss three different options and then choose the best.

8. The incentive scheme

Your company wants to offer incentives for good work but it doesn't want to give money away. Make a list of six incentives and then choose the best three ideas.

9. The TV show

A local TV company is making a series of programmes about companies in the region. It wants to film your company. It has asked you to make list of which parts of the company it ought to film and who it should interview. The programme is only 10 minutes long. Discuss the programme and plan the 10 minutes.

10. Improve security

Recently a person who is not employed by the company managed to enter the building and steal a laptop from someone's desk. Brainstorm different ways to make the building more secure. Then discuss and prepare a list of proposals.

> *"You can also give students different roles in a meeting. It ensures there is some difference of opinion and stimulates lively debate. Role playing meetings in a classroom setting is a great way for students to get hands-on experience."*
>
> **Richard Twigg, Director of Studies, International House Milan, Italy**

Unit 32

Unit 33

A telephone call can be on many different business-related topics and may require the students to be able to use a wide range of language. The call could take the form of a discussion or even a meeting if it's a teleconference with more than two speakers. So is there really a type of language that is specific to telephoning? Yes, but it's quite limited and it's usually taught to lower level students (elementary and pre-intermediate). Here are 10 sets of expressions that will be helpful to make some basic telephone calls in English. Your students may want to keep a copy of this list when making calls at work or doing telephone role plays in class.

1. Answering the phone

Hello?

Hello … [name] speaking.

[Company XYZ] Can I help you?

2. Introducing yourself

Hi. This is [name]

Hi, it's [name]

I'm with [name of the company]

I'm calling from [name of company]

3. Giving the reason

I'm calling to speak to …

I'm calling about …

The reason I'm calling is because …

4. Asking to speak to someone

Is [name] there?

Can I speak to …?

Could I talk to …?

5. Dealing with a caller

I'm not sure where he/she is at the moment.

One moment please.

Can you hold?

Can I get him/her to call you back?

She isn't at her desk but I can put you through to her voicemail.

6. Taking and leaving messages

Can I take a message? / Can I leave a message?

What's your name? / My name's …

What's your number? / It's …

What's it in connection with?

OK, I'll give him/her your message.

7. Checking and clarifying information

Can you repeat that?

So that's M for mother, A for apple…

Was that 17 or 70?

Did you say 17 or 70?

Seventeen. One, seven.

Let me read that back to you.

8. Dealing with a mistaken call

There's no one with that name here.

I think you've called the wrong [number/person].

Are you sure you've got the right [number/person/company]?

9. Dealing with technical problems

It's a really bad line.

You keep breaking up.

I'm on my mobile so I might lose you.

I lost you for a moment there. Can you repeat what you were saying?

10. Ending the call

I'm sorry but I must go.

Thanks for calling.

Nice speaking to you.

Bye for now.

Goodbye.

"The hardest part about using the telephone in a foreign language is that the conversation can begin anywhere, at any time, with no warning whatsoever. Suddenly, you have to start thinking in the new language, figure out who the other person is and try to hold some semblance of a normal conversation. One way to help students with this is to arrange for a colleague (e.g. another teacher) to call them during the lesson when they aren't expecting it. Monitor the call and give them feedback afterwards."

Alastair Lane, teacher and author, Barcelona

Unit 33

10 tips and telephone role plays

Once students have the basic language for telephoning (Unit 33), they will need lots and lots of practice and the most effective way to do this is to set up role plays. You'll find three key tips below followed by seven role plays you can use straight away or that you can adapt for your specific situation.

1. Classroom layout

If you work in a classroom where there are no phones or students are not allowed to use actual phones, students can sit at an angle to each other so they can't see the other person; this simulates the conditions of making a real phone call. However, if possible, use real phones in separate rooms or students could use their own mobiles.

2. Choice of role play

When choosing a role play to use with your students, you need to consider your aim. If it's to practice useful phrases for calling, then most role plays will do. If it's to practise certain target language such as time or dates then you'll need a situation where that language will occur. Finally, for students who have very specific needs, design the role play to reflect the types of calls they need to deal with.

3. Repeat the role play

Typically, a telephone role play is between Student A (the caller) and Student B (the person who answers). So after the role play is finished, it's always a good idea to have students switch roles and repeat the same role play. That way, both students have the chance to practise the language of both the caller and the person who answers. You can also repeat a role play after you have given feedback on the first attempt so that students can have another go at getting it right.

4. Dictating information

This role play is one of the simplest and is especially good for low level students. Give Student B a business card which contains the usual information such as a person's name, number, email, etc. Explain to Student A that they have lost the details of the person on the card so they call B to ask for the information; e.g. *Can you tell me his number? What's his email?* Student A can also ask B to repeat information or check certain words. Although the role play is not entirely realistic (B would probably email the information in reality), it is a great way to practice asking questions, speaking clearly, saying numbers, and spelling letters. Note that you could use the photocopiable business cards on p160 with this activity.

5. Arranging to meet

The aim is for Student A and B to arrange to meet. Ask them to make a schedule for the week with days, times and events written down. Make sure they both have busy schedules. (They could even use their real calendars on their phones.) A thinks of a reason to meet B and calls to arrange the meeting during the week. If you teach students in a large class, they can repeat the role play with a different partner and arrange another meeting and so on until they have made arrangements with a few people in the class.

Unit 34

6. A complaint

Give Student A the name of a household product (e.g. washing machine, TV, etc.) or give them a real item to hold. Explain that they have just bought this from a shop and arrived home only to find there is something wrong with it. (Alternatively they could have bought it online.) B works for the retailer and deals with customer enquiries and complaints. A calls B to complain about the item and must decide what action he/she wants B to take. B must resolve the situation.

7. Making a reservation

Explain that Student A has an important business visitor staying and wants to take him/her out for dinner. Give A the name of a restaurant – if you have the business card or menu of a restaurant even better. A must call B who works at the restaurant, and make a reservation for dinner. B should write down A's details.

8. Asking about travel information

Give Student B a piece of travel information such as a train or bus timetable. Tell Student A to call and find out about transport to certain places listed on the timetables. B reads for the relevant information and tells Student A. A writes it down. After the call, students should check that A wrote the correct information down.

9. A customer survey

We often use questionnaires or surveys in business so a useful context for a role play is to have Student A call B and explain that he/she is carrying out a customer survey for a business. A asks B the questions on the form. You can find sample customer survey forms online or students could create their own survey forms about their own business.

10. Recreate a recent call

One way to make the role play more relevant to students' own needs is for them to design a role play situation based on their own recent experience. Ask each student to think of a telephone call they recently made using English. They should note down answers to the following questions:

▶ What was the call about?

▶ Who answered?

▶ What was the outcome of the call?

Next put the students into pairs. They take turns to describe their call to each other. Then they try to recreate each of their calls.

"Ensure that you give your learners plenty of practice on answering the telephone. Have the students sit back-to-back to listen to each other, so they don't pick up on any paralinguistic features (facial clues, body language, gestures) as they listen."

Angela Buckingham, ELT writer and teacher trainer, UK

Unit 34

All presentations require students to be familiar with the content of what they want to say, and so your job is to help them with the specific vocabulary they might need. However, knowledge of the content doesn't guarantee an audience will follow you. Using language that structures the content is especially important. Many Business English books refer to this kind of language as 'signpost' phrases. In other words, it's the language that tells your audience what you are going to say next. Be prepared to teach students this type of language as a way to structure their ideas. Here is a list of the typical signpost phrases that students will find useful.

1. Welcome the audience

Good morning everyone.
Thank you for coming.
Thank you for inviting me.
My name's ... and I'm ...

2. Introduce the topic

Today, I'm going to be talking about...
The title of my presentation is...
I'd like to present ...
I've been asked to tell you about ...

3. Preview the structure of the talk

I'd like to begin with ...
Then we'll look at ...
Firstly / Secondly / Then / Next
And finally I'll talk about ...
I'll be happy to take questions at the end.
Feel free to ask questions during the presentation.

4. Move forward to the next point

That brings me to my next point.
Let's move on to ...
Moving on to ... / Turning to ...

5. Refer to visual aids

As you can see from the table...
Take a look at this graph.
I'd like to show you some statistics ...
This chart shows ...

6. Refer back to a previous point

As I was saying earlier ...
Going back to what I said about ...
This refers back to ...

7. Explain and exemplify

Let me explain in more detail.
I'd like to spend a few minutes explaining how ...
This is a good example of ...
For example, ...

8. Summing up and concluding

To sum up, ...
In conclusion, ...
So, overall ...
That brings me to the end of the presentation.

9. Inviting and handling questions

I'll take some questions now.
Any questions?
That's a good question.
Thank you for your question.
I'm sorry, I don't think I quite follow.
Can you repeat your question?

10. Thank everyone and say goodbye

That's all we have time for.
If you'd like to contact me, my email is ...
Thanks for listening.

Unit 35

"Ensure students use signposting language to help them focus and maintain a structure, while at the same time enabling the audience to follow coherently."

Kat Robb, Business English teacher, Spain

As with any communication skill in a Business English class, you will want to give feedback on correct and effective use of language. However, giving an effective presentation requires more than just making error-free sentences. As you become more experienced as a Business English teacher you can also comment on other areas of presenting to help students become more effective or invite students to give their own peer feedback. Here are 10 areas for providing feedback.

1. Language

When noting areas to give feedback on, focus in particular on whether the student uses key content vocabulary correctly. For example, if the presentation is about a particular topic then clearly the subject-specific vocabulary needs to be used correctly and pronounced so that everyone will understand.

2. Signposting

This follows on from giving feedback on language in 1. If you have been teaching the students to use some of the signpost language needed for presenting (see Unit 35), then you will give positive feedback on correct usage and also give remedial help where signpost language is not used correctly (or not used at all).

3. Rapport with audience

Clearly, not all students feel at ease with presenting and this often inhibits their ability to build a relationship with their audience. You can give tips such as shaking people's hands when they arrive or chatting to members of the audience while waiting to begin. This can break the ice and make both presenter and audience feel at ease. Reminding students to smile at the beginning can also help with rapport.

4. Eye contact and body language

Part of rapport-building (see 3) involves looking directly at your audience when speaking and not up at the ceiling or towards the slides. You may need to tell a student to do this in your feedback. A presenter's body language can also affect how the audience responds; any gesture with the hands should have purpose. Similarly, when a presenter walks around there should be a reason; aimless walking is very distracting.

5. Introduction

A well-structured presentation will begin with an introduction. A safe way to start is to say things like who you are and who you work for if your audience don't know you, and to say what your talk is going to be about. At a more advanced level you could also start to suggest adding techniques like storytelling or asking your audience a question and getting a show of hands; e.g. *How many of you clicked on an online advert before you arrived here today?*

6. Navigating the main content

The longest and most complex part of the presentation will be the middle section with all the key content. For technical presentations in particular you will need to help students guide their audience through the different stages. This includes using signpost language, but it might also require simplifying explanations depending on the knowledge-level of the audience. In this case you will need to feed in ideas for adjusting the English but at the same time not changing the content so it becomes too simplified or even untrue.

7. Visual aids

Be prepared to give plenty of feedback on this area. Inexperienced presenters (and some experienced) have a tendency to use too many slides with too much information on. They might read long sentences from their slides and lose the interest of their audience. It's worth asking your students to send you copies of their slides beforehand for inspection and feedback. Some general tips to give are not to have more than five bullet points with text per slide and, where possible, replace text with a picture or image. For presenting graphs, charts and technical information, only include the key data that you plan to refer to.

8. Delivery

You will need to tell students to speak up if they are too quiet (or use a microphone) and project their voice to the back of the audience. This might involve working on students' pronunciation skills including using stress and pauses effectively to get their point across. (See Unit 42, activity 9.)

9. Concluding

At the end, the audience needs to know what they should do as a result of listening to the presentation. So a conclusion must announce the end of the presentation but also a summing up of the key points and what action should be taken. If this isn't clear, work on this with the student.

10. Handling questions

Many students remark that the final stage of a presentation scares them most because they can prepare the main presentation but they can't predict what the audience might ask them. Set aside time in the lesson for the audience to ask questions so the student gets practice at handling questions. It's useful to give them phrases like *That's a good question, Sorry can you repeat your question?* or *Let me check I've understood your question…*

▶▶ **See p163 for a photocopiable feedback form to use or adapt for your presentation skills classes.**

10 tips for organising in-class presentations

When you ask students to give presentations in class you will need other students to listen and act as the audience. It is of course an opportunity for these students to develop their listening skills but at the same time it can create classroom management difficulties. For example, students who are waiting to give presentations afterwards will find it hard to concentrate. Students might find it hard to understand each other or simply not find someone's presentation very interesting. Here are 10 tips on setting up these kinds of in-class presentations so that they are as useful for the students in the audience as much as for the presenter.

1. Presentations per lesson

Many of your students will want to develop their presentation skills but if everyone presents in the same lesson it can take up lots of time and be hard to maintain everyone's concentration. As a general rule, it's a good idea to spread presentations over a series of lessons if you can. For example, set aside time in each lesson for two or three; that's the right amount to keep everyone interested and students often like the mixture of the 'normal' lesson and watching their peers present.

2. Set time limits

Following on from the issue of time in tip 1, it's also wise to set clear time limits and ensure students to stick to them. Don't allow students to run over a time limit for presentation because it will irritate other students. You will need to be firm, but if you stop students when they overrun early on in the course they will soon learn to control their timekeeping.

3. Set comprehension questions

If you are familiar with the content of the presenter's talk, then prepare a set of comprehension questions for the audience which they have to answer during the presentation.

4. Create three questions

Instead of writing comprehension questions yourself, tell the students in the audience the title of the presentation and say a few words about the general topic. Then ask them to write down three questions before the talk that they expect the presenter to answer. During the presentation itself, students in the audience listen out for answers to their questions and note them down. At the end, if any of their questions remained unanswered, they can ask them at the end.

5. Noting the key points

Ask the listening students to write down the main points that they think the presenter wants them to take away from the talk. At the end, ask students to compare with a partner what they noted down. Students should notice any differences between what they focused on and why. It can also be helpful for the presenter to receive feedback on what other students noted down as it tells them if they managed to get their key message across.

6. Allocate tasks

When running in-class presentations there can be a few different things to manage so allocate them out to students. For example, you might set time limits on a presentation so one student in the audience could be in charge of timekeeping and signal to a speaker when their time is about to run out. We often video presentations so put a student in charge of filming it.

7. Filling in peer feedback forms

Unit 36 looks at what to include in a feedback form for business presentation skills and how to use the form effectively. The same form, or similar, can of course be completed by peers, although you may need to simplify them or at least clarify exactly how to complete it.

8. One thing I liked was ...

If you think that using long feedback forms will be overly complex – especially early on in a course – then simplify the observation task like this: ask students while watching, or at the end, to write down one thing they really liked about their peer's presentation and one suggestion they have for improvement. Then set aside a little bit of time for feedback to be given at the end.

9. Students choose an observation point

As a variation to tips 7 and 8, ask each student in the audience to write down one area of presenting that they are currently trying to improve and work on. So they might write down *'Making clear introductions and conclusions'* or *'Using eye contact effectively'*. Explain that they must watch the presentation and consider how the presenter copes with this area. They don't necessarily give any feedback but instead they think about whether the presenter did or didn't handle that area successfully. If they observed a successful demonstration they can learn from this person how to improve their own presentations. On the other hand, if the presenter demonstrates the same difficulty, then the observer might be able to recognise what is causing it and apply the conclusions to their own presenting.

10. A buddy system

Because presenting can be stressful, you could pair up students so that on one day when one of them presents, the other partner is their 'buddy'. He or she is responsible for helping the presenter with any basic preparation such as arranging for the all the technology to be set up correctly, dealing with any last minute hitches and possibly be the person primarily responsible for giving peer feedback. Obviously, you'll need to pair up students sensitively or even let them select their own partner.

Unit 37

We often associate the skill of negotiating with high level executives sitting in board rooms arguing over the finer points of a multi-million dollar takeover or merger. In fact, the majority of negotiating in business takes place at a much more day-to-day level. Students needs the language and skills for negotiating when they place an order, discuss the length of time a delivery might take, try to find ways to decrease their manufacturing costs, or even ask for a pay rise. It's a difficult skill in any language, so carrying it out in English is a real challenge for your students. Here are 10 sets of phrases you could give to your students which are organised in the way a negotiation might be structured. Note that some stages might be longer or shorter depending on the types of negotiation.

1. Starting

I'd like to discuss …
We have an issue with the (price/contract/delivery times, etc.)
Can we talk about the terms of …?

2. State your position

Our position is that …
I'm not able to accept …
My concern is that …

3. Find out about the other side's position

What do you think about …?
What's your position on this?
Do you have any concerns with …?

4. Checking everyone has understood

So if I've understood you correctly, you'd like …
Let's check we understand each other's position.
You're asking for …

5. Making an offer

We can offer …
I'd like to propose that …
In return, you'd give us …

6. Refusing the offer

I'm sorry but that isn't acceptable.
I'm afraid that's too [high/low, etc.]
That isn't possible for us.

7. Making a counter offer

We would be able to …

I couldn't accept [X], but I might be able to accept [Y].

How about if we were to offer you … instead

8. Compromising

We might be able to reduce [the price].

Can we reach a compromise?

There's some room for manoeuvre on this.

As a compromise, we could … if you …

9. Agreeing

We can probably agree to that.

I think that would be OK.

That's agreed.

10. Confirming what has been agreed

So let's just sum up what we've agreed (so far).

Firstly, we've agreed that … Secondly, we've also agreed that …

I'll confirm what we've agreed by email.

Unit38

"Lawyers, doctors, business people, teachers and police officers all negotiate. This vital skill is hard in the native language and it needs to be taught in a supportive and focused manner in a second language."

Christopher Graham, Business English Trainer, London

10 tips on a negotiating lesson

Negotiating is a challenging skill to deal with in your classes but if it's handled well, students will really throw themselves into a well-staged negotiation lesson. Here are 10 tips and ideas to get you started.

1. Mixed ability English

Note that students with quite low levels of English can often be more effective at negotiating than students with higher levels of English. In fact, some students even use their lack of English to their advantage by pretending that they didn't understand an important point because of their English, when in fact they understood perfectly well! It's all part of the skill that goes into getting the best deal. So when you set up a role play situation in class it isn't always necessary to pair or group students according to their level of English. For negotiating, you might sort the students according to their ability to drive a hard bargain.

2. The win-win scenario

It is often said that there are three possible outcomes for the two sides in any negotiation:

▶ Win-lose: One side gets a better deal while the other side leaves disappointed.

▶ Lose-lose: The negotiation falls apart because no one can agree so both sides leave with nothing.

▶ Win-win: Both sides leave the negotiation with a solution they feel happy with.

In most cases, the final win-win outcome is usually considered the preferable outcome because it leads to a better long-term business relationship between the two sides. However, some of your students might aim for a win-lose option in which they try to get the most from a deal. You could lead into any lesson on negotiating by discussing these three outcomes and asking your students these questions: *Which outcome do you think is better and why? Which type of outcome have you experienced in a negotiation? What happened?*

3. Introducing the stages and language for negotiating

You could hand out the sets of stages and useful phrases in Unit 38 to each student. Alternatively, use a recording of a negotiation (or make your own) and ask students to listen and make notes on what each side wants from the deal. Students could also listen and note down the stages and useful phrases they hear.

4. A quick negotiation scenario

For shorter lessons or setting up quick ways to practise a negotiation, choose some obvious types of day-to-day negotiations that don't require any specialist knowledge. Here's an example. As a class, brainstorm and write on the board the types of household tasks that people generally don't like doing. These might include: *washing-up, vacuuming, cleaning the bathroom, cleaning the windows, doing the grocery shopping*, etc.

Next, put students into pairs and explain that they now rent a small apartment together. They must draw up an agreement on how the household jobs will be shared out between them both fairly. As they negotiate they should make notes because at the end each pair has to present what they agreed. Note that they are not allowed to hire someone to do the work for them!

5. Thinking about and planning your position

When you ask students to negotiate in class it's very important that they are given time to plan their position. For example, in the previous suggestion (see activity 4) for a negotiation over household chores, the activity will probably be more effective if students have a few minutes to think about which jobs they want to do and don't want to do so they are ready to argue their position. With more extended negotiations that are more complex it's even helpful to stop the negotiation sometimes so that students can reflect on and perhaps reconsider their position. This kind of silent thinking time is also a chance to prepare the kind of language they might need.

6. Extended negotiations

For more extensive, and perhaps more realistic, negotiation practice you will need to provide students with details of the situation. For example, if you set up a classic scenario where the management of a firm are negotiating working conditions with trade union representatives then you will need to create fictional details outlining the employee's current salaries, weekly working hours, length of breaks, number of holidays per year and so on. You can also use the photocopiable negotiation brief on p164 to set this activity up.

This kind of negotiation often works better if you allow for the negotiation to take place in different stages and put the students into teams of two or three per side. So the lesson might look like this:

▶ The two sides (managers and employees) receive their details and discuss their position in separate parts of the classroom.

▶ Both sides come together and present their positions and start to discuss what they might or might not accept.

▶ The two sides take a break and work separately to discuss what they might counter offer or compromise on.

▶ The two sides come back to each other and continue the negotiation until they reach a final agreement.

Note that the discussion time between members working on the same side is as productive and important as the negotiating time with the other side in this kind of task.

7. The teacher's role

Once you have introduced the language for negotiating and set up the role play scenario, you should take a back seat. Observe the stages and make notes about the language used and what went well or not so well for each side in the task. During a negotiation, if for some reason one side is having difficulty or the negotiation is not moving forward, you can intervene. For example, if a group has taken a break from talking to the other side and is planning their next move, then you could join them and make suggestions about their strategy or provide them with the language they might need.

8. Student reflection on the task

After an extended negotiation, set aside time for the students to comment on how they think the negotiation went. You could write these two questions on the board to guide their comments:

▶ What kind of outcome do you think achieved? (e.g. win-win, win-lose, lose, lose).

▶ What went well? If you did it again, what would you do differently next time?

Allow time for everyone to comment on their own performance.

9. Your feedback

After students have commented on the negotiation (see activity 8), give your own feedback. If you feel students have picked out the key issues relating to their negotiation strategy then focus on giving them feedback on the language they used or make suggestions on language they might use next time.

10. Repeat the negotiation

Having reflected on the negotiation and the language used, it's worth asking students to repeat the role play or at least do a similar negotiation to try and improve their performance. It's also interesting to have students swap roles and try to negotiate from the position of the other side, although it's worth changing some of the details so no one is familiar with the exact position of the other side.

"For the Business English learner confidence is key. So build repeated activities into the course where their improvement can be demonstrably shown."

Paul Dummett, Business English trainer and author

Unit 39

Business language skills

This final section of Business English ETpedia brings together a range of areas which are all broadly linked to teaching students English with an emphasis on business. If you already have experience of teaching English in the General English classroom then you will be familiar with many of the basic principles in this section. For example, the first three units (40 to 42) look at teaching grammar, vocabulary and pronunciation. The difference is that they consider how we adapt these key areas to relate to a business context. So the ideas for teaching grammar all reflect a business context or the pronunciation activities relate to business communication skills.

The next three units (43 to 45) focus on business writing. Arguably, business writing can be considered as a type of communication skill, but it also tends to be taught with a lot of focus on vocabulary and improving writing sub-skills. The written text is also the main focus of units 46 and 47 because it addresses the importance of authentic materials which you can adapt and use in your lessons. You'll also find suggestions on using authentic listenings and unit 47 suggests exercises and activities that work well in lessons with reading or listenings.

During a course you will probably want to test your student from time to time and towards the end some of your students might be interested in (or required to) take a formal examinations. The final two units in this section look at the area of testing and examinations in Business English.

Although learning grammar on a Business English course isn't always the top priority for many students, you will still need to teach it in the same way you would on a general English course. The trick is to try and teach and practise it within a relevant business or work-related context. Here are 10 contexts and activities you can try for some of the most commonly taught grammar points.

1. Present simple with work routines

Ask students to work on their own and draw a pie chart which shows what proportion of their working day they spend on different activities. You could draw this one as an example to illustrate what you mean:

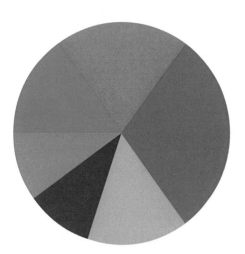

- Deal with emails (15%)
- Attend meetings (20%)
- Talk to customers (30%)
- Eat and take breaks (15%)
- Do paperwork (10%)
- Talk to colleagues next to my desk (10%)

Students draw their pie charts and then present their chart to a partner or in small groups using the present simple to describe their routines. The listening students should be encouraged to ask questions for more details such as *What time do you take your breaks?*

(Also see Unit 19, tip 6 for more practise with the present simple for routines.)

2. Past simple and present perfect for company/career history

All your students will have a career history and the company itself will have a timeline which can be described with key events. Start by writing some dates on the board. Depending on the age of your class you should put up dates at five year intervals going back in time. They should be in a vertical line moving downwards towards the current year like this:

	1975	
1981 Thomas qualified	1980	
1989 Sara got married	1985	
	1990	*1991 Sam started work here*
1999 Juan joined IBM	1995	*1998 Hugo left university*
	2000	*2003 Marie graduated*
2004 Sofia got her first job	2005	
	2010	*2011 Eduardo became a manager*
	2015	

Next ask the class to write down some key moments in their lives along with the year and then discuss them with a partner. The partner reports back and the events are written at the appropriate point on the board, *Hugo left university in 1998. Sofia got her first job in 2004.* You will soon have a board full of facts which will allow the group to practise simple past questions and answers and potentially the Present Perfect. Students ask each other questions such as *When did Juan join the company? When did Marie graduate? How long has Sam worked here?* The level of the group will determine how complex the sentences can be. Company histories work in the same way and can be found online or the class can piece them together from their own knowledge.

3. Future forms with business predictions

Whatever the professional activity of your students they will be able to make predictions about their company, their industry and their country. A simple activity is to write time clauses *in a few years, by the time I retire, when my kids are adults* or *future years, 2020, 2030,* etc. on cards and ask them to work in groups or pairs and make predictions such as *'In 2025 we will have more robots than people in the factory'.* Their ideas can be qualified with adverbs like *definitely, possibly, probably* – *'In 2025 we will **probably** have more robots than people in the factory'.* From these basic predictions you can correct and improve their language to make more complex sentences with *I think, I don't think, I guess, in my opinion* etc. *'I think that in 2025 we will **probably** have more robots than people in the factory'.*

(Also see Unit 34, activity 5 for practising future forms in the context of arranging to meet.)

4. Conditionals – business contexts

An activity which encourages students to use and practise conditional sentences is to look at a present situation and compare it to the future. Use the board to illustrate or project an image of a factory which currently produces 3,000 cars a week. Elicit what the production numbers for next week are. Practise the sentence –'*If there are no problems we will produce 3,000 cars next week.*' Add more information to create a new sentence each time. Draw on the board a happy manager and elicit, '*If they produce 3,000 cars the manager will be happy*'. Draw on the board a broken machine and elicit, '*If there is a breakdown they will produce fewer cars*'. These sentences are all 1st conditional because the events are quite possible. 2nd conditional sentences introduce less probable events such as opening a second factory, increasing productivity by 20%, doubling wages, etc. and elicit sentences like, '*If we opened a second factory we could produce 6,000 cars a week.*' As a follow-up, give the class some problems (see suggestions below) and get them to come up with solutions using either of the conditional forms above.

The waiting list for cars is nine months.

We can't find enough staff.

We don't make a large enough profit.

(Also see Unit 39, activity 6 for practising using conditional forms in the context of a negotiation.)

5. Infinitive and gerunds with interests and small talk

In one of your first lessons with a new class you will probably discuss their likes and dislikes, whether talking about aspects of their job, their pastimes or their family. In a large group, mingling activities work very well. Give the class a handout where they have to find one person for each of the following:

Someone with an interesting hobby.

Someone with an interesting job.

Someone's dream holiday.

ETpedia: 500 ideas for Business English teachers © Pavilion Publishing and Media Ltd and its licensors 2016. **111**

Unit 40

Someone who makes interesting food.

Someone who likes an unusual sport.

Someone who would like to try another job.

Someone with interesting plans for the weekend.

Someone who dislikes a particular form of transport.

When they report back they will use language like *Hugo hates flying. Sara would love to visit Brazil. Karl loves diving. Peter enjoys doing research. Juliet is looking forward to going to Edinburgh.*

6. Modal verbs in rules and advice

If you are teaching in-company then you are in an excellent position to have some of the rules explained to you: *Staff have to start by 9.30 at the latest. We have to do a minimum of 37 hours a week. We don't have to wear special clothes. In the open plan offices, you shouldn't talk too loud.* You can then transfer these modals to the classroom and set up some guidelines for your class to do in connection to the following: speaking English, doing homework, taking part in activities, etc. As a group they can decide on six rules for successful English learning.

(Also see Unit 15, activity 8 for more practice with modal verbs in the context of giving rules.)

7. Comparatives and superlatives for talking about products

Finding out about the products and services your students are involved in is a natural way of practising comparatives and superlatives. Write a table on the board with key information about three products including details about size, weight, price and other features. You can also use the photocopiable table on p166. Ask students to write in the details of one of their company's products and then add information about two competing products. With pre-work students or students who don't have products, ask them to research three competing products for homework such as three different types of mobile phones. They can quickly find this kind of information on price comparison websites.

The next stage is for students to present their three products to a partner and summarise the main differences using sentences with comparative or superlative forms. For example: *Our model is lighter/more efficient/less complicated than this one. It's also the cheapest.* You could also make this an information gap activity by giving the student who is listening the task of filling in a blank table about the three products.

8. Determiners and nouns – eating out

Among the grammar words which students have to learn, determiners are often overlooked because they rarely lead to a breakdown in communication. You cannot teach them all in one go, but the situation of placing orders in a restaurant gives an opportunity to deal with quite a few. It is also a situation which all students enjoy practising. To set up your restaurant context you can brainstorm some restaurant vocabulary; *chairs, tables, waiter, plates, glasses, cutlery.* Then, depending on the level, you can practise the following:

this, that, these, those	*Can we have that table?*
some, any, no	*Would you like any drinks?*

all, each, every	*All the desserts are great!*
both, either, neither	*Still or sparkling? Either, I really don't mind.*
much, many, a little, a few, a lot	*Peas? Just a few, please.*
enough, too much/many	*I think I've eaten enough.*

The dialogue can be built up and practised by the class, giving a nice context for the determiner focus.

9. Passive form for describing factory processes

When describing processes we tend to use the passive form, for example, '*The bricks are manufactured here and then they are transported in lorries …*'. Assuming you have presented the passive form to students, try to find visual representations of processes. You'll find many diagrams showing processes online or students may have their own which they can present. In addition, there are videos on YouTube showing processes or some companies also have their own films about their processes which you can show in class with the sound off and ask students to narrate them. (Also see Unit 26, activity 6 for more ideas on using the passive form with process language.)

10. Question forms about a company profile

You'll find lots of activities in this resource that offer the opportunity for students to practise using questions. However, for low level speaking practice, use the photocopiable activity on p167. Students work in pairs with one copy (cut in half) between them. They each have different information about a company and take turns to ask and answer questions to complete the company profile. Note that you could design your own version of this activity by finding out about real companies from their websites or you could even base it on your students' own companies. You can also increase the difficulty of the task by adding more information to the company profiles. As a follow-up activity for higher level students, ask them to visit the company website for homework and prepare more questions. Then they swap their questions with a partner and try to find the answers on the website.

"While it's true that minor grammar errors (like: 'We're received your order yesterday.') often don't impede communication, it's important to bear in mind that learners' own reputations, and that of their companies are at stake. Accuracy is often inextricably bound up with questions of face."

Brian Brennan, Language Training Manager, Barcelona

Unit 40

Unit 41

Vocabulary is a key part of teaching Business English and many of your students will want a larger active vocabulary so they can talk about their own area of business or work as well as more general topics. Here are 10 ways to help them build their vocabulary.

1. Mind-maps and brainstorming

Mind-mapping and brainstorming are very useful for generating vocabulary. You can use the technique in class and students can develop it as a study skill. Here's an example of a mind-map for the word *security* which the teacher has brainstormed with students on the board:

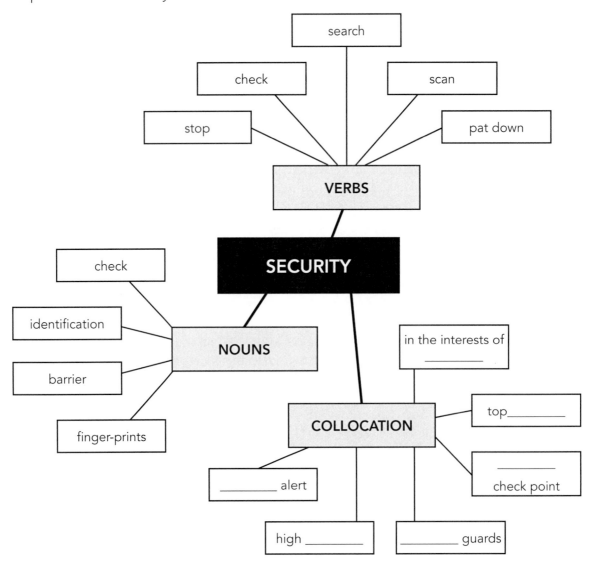

2. Word-building

When students find a new word, encourage them to find other forms of it; for example, build words out from a headword like organise including *organise, organised, disorganised, organisation*. See the photocopiable word-building table on p168. You can give a copy to each student and they add new words when they find them.

3. Jumbled letters

Another way of revising words which have been recently taught is to jumble the letters up and ask the class to unscramble them to find the word. A lesson on jobs might feature these words:

1. drocot	2. tiplo	3. riubled	4. rouaidt	5. ledmo
6. revidr	7. cheater	8. ysvrreou	9. gnrnieee	10. tljsunioar

(Answers: *1. doctor 2. pilot 3. builder 4. auditor 5. model 6. driver 7. teacher 8. surveyor 9.engineer 10. journalist*)

4. Missing letters

Getting students to guess words with some letters missing is also a good way to practise vocabulary. You can remove the vowels, the consonants, or simply the first and last letters. In this example of office words the first and last letters are missing.

1. _il_	2. _es_	3._am_	4. _hon_	5. _ape_
6. _hai_	7. _oo_	8. _ous_	9. _e_	10. _arpe_

(Answers: *1. file 2. desk 3. lamp 4. phone 5. paper 6. chair 7. door 8. mouse 9. pen 10. carpet*)

5. Crosswords and word searches

Puzzle books with crosswords and word searches are very popular with many people and so they can be a motivating activity for practising vocabulary. You can construct your own crossword using an online crossword maker. Word searches are equally easy to make. Using a 10 x 10 grid put in eight or more words you have taught recently with the words running horizontally, vertically, diagonally or backwards. Fill in all the other squares with random letters. See an example of a ready-to-use photocopiable word search on p169.

6. Team games

You can turn vocabulary activities into team games. Words can be written on pieces of card or paper and students have to pick a word and define it to their side of the class. If they cannot guess it, the other side can try for a bonus point. An alternative is to have students sitting in front of the board where a number of words are projected or written. Their colleagues have to define them so they can guess them. Team games can also be based on a student miming the word or drawing a picture of it so the team members can guess what it is.

7. Memory game

One easy activity is to place around 20 objects on a tray or in a box and give the class one minute to look. They then have two minutes to name all the items they have seen. One way of helping them remember is if they try and invent a story which links the objects. Another memory game is to try and build a list of words in order. So one student begins like this: '*Today I have to arrange some training*'. The next students says something like: '*Today I have to arrange some training, and book some tickets.*' And so it continues with students making the list of activities longer and longer and trying to remember all the items.

Unit 41

ETpedia: 500 ideas for Business English teachers © Pavilion Publishing and Media Ltd and its licensors 2016.

115

8. Gap fill the target vocabulary

Take a text and gap-fill 10 of the nouns. Hand it out to students and ask them to work in pairs to work out what the missing words might be. There will be contextual clues to help them, but not necessarily only one correct answer. This ability to work out the meaning from the text around is a very useful skill. To make it easier you could provide the missing words above the text or you could turn it into a multiple choice activity so students have options for each gap.

9. Alphabet game

Using the photocopiable activity on p170 (or draw the table on the board and have students copy it), students have to think of words starting with a letter in different topics or categories. Students can either think of words on their own, in pairs or in teams of three. They have a time limit and can win points so it's fun and competitive. It's also excellent revision practice.

10. Personalise the word

With any new word it's worth asking students to try and use the word in a sentence which is personal to them or relevant to their work. It's useful in any English class but in a Business English class it's especially useful because you are encouraging students to make the vocabulary needs-related.

"Business English learners can use a vocabulary box containing blank index cards. They write a new word or phrase on the front of a card and write a personalised sentence with the new vocabulary in context on the back, or a translation. Students can use these cards to revise, and discard each card when the vocabulary item is learnt. An app like 'Quizlet' allows students to create digital cards on a Smartphone, tablet or PC, and then recycle sets of words by playing a matching game. Students can also store words in concept groups on a dictionary app, creating suitable topic areas such as 'marketing' or 'finance'."

Pete Sharma, Business English teacher, teacher trainer and author, UK

10 tips and activities for pronunciation in Business English

When you carry out a needs analysis with your students (see Units 9 and 10), they will often request work on their speaking skills, which means you will have to take into consideration the issue of pronunciation. In fact, some students might even say they want to sound like a native speaker or that they will be happy as long as they are intelligible to their counterparts. Some students will not be aware that their pronunciation is affecting their business communication skills so you will need to address this issue early on in the course.

1. Balancing accuracy and fluency

Teaching pronunciation is often associated with improving accuracy; conversely, there is also a common myth that the average Business English learner is more interested in being fluent than in being accurate. It is true that often a busy manager has little time to study, and so opts for intensive language training, which doesn't lend itself to improving pronunciation in the same way that an extended course (over a year or more) might. Instead, the learner aims for communicative competence: as long as the message is communicated, the details of correct grammar or pronunciation are subsidiary.

2. Using pronunciation to be more effective

However, in Business English teaching we are also interested in effectiveness – how well is the message put across to the listener? Is the listener convinced by our message? Effectiveness is the total performance (linguistic and non-linguistic). In pronunciation terms, effectiveness might be extra stress placed on a key word to add emphasis or a meaningful pause to make an audience reflect.

3. Student interest

Aside from the more pedagogical reasoning for having pronunciation on the Business English syllabus, students tend to enjoy working on pronunciation. They recognise its importance, especially when enduring long periods of listening or the stress of making even the briefest personal introduction in English.

4. Business vocabulary stress

Whenever you teach a new word with more than one syllable, make it a habit to mark the stress on the word and have students do the same. Say the word aloud and ask them to repeat it and say where they think the stress falls. You can also use the photocopiable Word Stress worksheet on p171 to help students develop the habit of recognising word stress.

5. Telephoning and connected speech

There are no visual cues on the telephone, so students don't have the luxury of interpreting meaning from a facial expression or shift of the body. To help with listening to telephone calls, select a listening that you have already used in the lesson. Choose some of the sentences from the recording and read them at natural speed or play the extracts from the recording. Ask the students to identify how many words are in the sentence. For example: Teacher: *Can I leave a message?* Student: *Five words.* Teacher: *He's out of the office.* Student: *Five words.* (Note that contracted forms count as one word.) Teacher: *I'm afraid he's out of the office.* Student: *Seven words.* This technique focuses students on how the 'little words' (*a, of,* etc.) get lost, and it develops their confidence with listening.

ETpedia: 500 ideas for Business English teachers © Pavilion Publishing and Media Ltd and its licensors 2016.

Unit 42

6. Using contrastive stress

In business, when dealing with lots of figures and details, speakers often use contrastive stress to check and clarify meaning. So while your learners might be happy to say '*Sorry, can you repeat that?*' when they are unsure of some information, they also need to be aware of how words are sometimes stressed to check and clarify. For example:

A: *So your final figure is five hundred?*

B: *No, nine hundred.*

To practise this feature, use the photocopiable dominoes on p172. You'll need one copy for each group (two to four students per group). Cut up the dominoes. Follow the set of instructions given or let the group read and try to understand them. Students will match the dominoes first by context and then by how the underlined syllable or word is given prominent stress.

7. Strategy building

Following on from activity 6, students will need to build other strategies for clarifying their pronunciation. This is especially true for areas using spelling and numbers. One lower level activity when you introduce the alphabet for the first time is to have students think of a word that begins with each letter and use it for clarifying when spelling. You can also give them themes to follow such as the names of countries and cities; for example, '*A as in Amsterdam, B as in Berlin, C as in Canada.*' They can create a list and use it when dictating information to each other (see Unit 34 activity 4). Another strategy with saying numbers is to have students use techniques for breaking the numbers down; for example: '*The number is 13, as in one three.*' Tips for strategies such as these can really help students early on when they are struggling with their pronunciation.

8. Meetings and sentence stress

Moving the stress in a sentence is a technique commonly used in meetings and negotiations to change emphasis or meaning. If your students have been listening to a meeting, choose one of the phrases used and write it on the board. Read out the sentence, stressing one word in particular. Ask the students to underline it. Now read it again, changing the stressed word and ask the students to underline it again. This can be repeated as many times as there are words. For example:

1. *What's your opinion?*

2. *What's your opinion?*

3. *What's your opinion?*

9. Presentations and pausing

To help the delivery of a presentation, presenters often use pauses in certain places. Typically, you'll hear a pause where there are full stops and commas, so pausing acts like a kind of punctuation and helps an audience follow. However, you can also put pauses around important information such as the name of a company or important numbers and figures. Try reading this extract from a presentation aloud and pause where you see this symbol /.

Good morning everyone, / and thank you for coming. Today, / I'd like talk about / Fowler / Plastics / Limited / and our results for the years / 2015 / to 2016.

You can demonstrate the same thing to students by writing the extract on the board but leave out the pauses. Then read it aloud with the pauses and ask students to note down where you paused. Then discuss the reasons why you paused where you did. Next, ask students to choose a few sentences from a presentation they have given and write in where they think the pauses sound natural and effective. Finally, they can work in pairs and take turns to read their sentences aloud to each other and see if the pauses are effective.

10. Intonation to add interest

Spoken business communication is often about keeping the listener's interest. Flat-sounding intonation is monotonous and will, for example, lose an audience's attention in a presentation. To highlight this to a student take any short stretch of speech such as part of a presentation a student is working on. Read it aloud with very flat intonation and then read it again with rising and falling intonation. Ask the student to tell you what the different was between each reading. They should notice that the first reading was less interesting because of the dull intonation.

"The aim of learning English for business should be comfortable intelligibility, both speaking and listening. There is no 'correct' pronunciation, but there is lesser and greater intelligibility. Whenever learning and practising a new language, it is not enough to attend only to the grammar or vocabulary, because how it is said and heard is an integral part of it, and can be practised at the same time. Integrate pronunciation purposefully all the time with everything."

Adrian Underhill, trainer and author, UK

Unit 42

Unit 43

It's very hard to predict the types of writing that students might have to write themselves so you will need to ask them as part of their needs analysis and try to get examples of the kind of texts they deal with. The following texts are some of the most likely that a student might have to write. You would probably include them on a course for pre-work students but they might also form the basis of a list for in-work students to choose from on a needs analysis form.

1. Emails

An unimaginable number of emails are sent to and from businesses every second of every day around the world. Virtually all of your students will have to read and write emails relating to their work and many will ask you for help with them. If most of your class time is devoted to speaking practice, then have students email their work to you for feedback. You can even email them a fictional work-related email to which they have to respond.

2. Letters

Although the primary form of correspondence is email, people do still send and receive letters in envelopes or by fax in this day and age. These might include a formal letter of resignation, a letter of application, a reference, a marketing letter, etc. In many cases, the language of the letter will be similar to the language used in emails (see Unit 44 for phrases) though they may be more formal and follow stricter conventions (see Unit 45). As with practising emails, you can write a letter which a student must reply to.

3. Personal profiles and biodata

At lower levels, it can be useful to help students write a short paragraph outlining who they are, what they do and their responsibilities. Increasingly, we have to write this kind of short personal profile to appear on social media pages such as LinkedIn or perhaps as biodata to be printed in a conference booklet. If you ever set up a class website, students can introduce themselves like this online.

4. Notes

Taking notes in English is a particular skill because it is often about writing while listening to people talking; for example, listening to a discussion in a meeting or noting down the key points of a presentation. In class, students can listen to recordings, take notes and then compare what they have written down with a partner. Alternatively, if your students have role played a meeting, assign the job of taking notes on what was said to one student in the group and have them write up the minutes of the meeting.

5. Reports

Teaching report writing can be challenging because the style and format of a report can vary from company to company. As with any type of business or work-related writing, you should also ask your students to show you examples of the types of reports they have to deal with. Report-writing is also tested in some exams and as a general rule your students will need to make use of headings such as *Introduction, Terms of reference, Findings, Conclusion and recommendations*.

6. Instructions

Some students, especially those dealing with machinery or processes, might have to write short instructions for others. One fun way to do this is to have each student write a set of real instructions for a process like finding a particular room in the building or making a paper aeroplane. Once they have written the instructions they swap them with a partner who must try to follow the instructions. It's a useful test of whether the writing is comprehensible. (See also Unit 22.)

7. Slides (for a presentation)

Part of helping students to develop presentation skills is working on their ability to use visual aids well. This includes writing information on their slides in English. For example, they might list a series of bullet points to summarise the key issues in their talk. As we generally avoid writing whole sentences on a slide, students will need help with shortening their sentences into bullet points.

8. Filling in forms

A surprising amount of time is spent nowadays filling in forms online such as applying for travel visas, ordering something online, registering to receive information from a company, or an job application form. It can be a useful area of writing to look at with lower level students who are learning to write single words and personal information, as well as helping students with specific needs that involve form filling.

9. Questionnaires and surveys

As well as filling in forms (see 8) you might also work with students who create forms such as online questionnaires and surveys. For example, a marketing department might want to carry out a customer survey or perhaps a manager wants an internal questionnaire for staff feedback. This kind of writing is also good practice of question forms. Students can create their own online surveys using free web-based tools like www.surveymonkey.com. Once they have created their own form, their classmates can fill it in (and give feedback on their English of course!)

10. CV/Resume

Many of your pre-work students at college or university will benefit from help in writing their CVs in English, but you may also be asked by in-work students who are thinking of applying for new job. See Unit 21 for suggestions on the area of applying for a job.

10 sets of useful phrases for writing emails and correspondence

When it comes to writing for business, the majority of your students will receive and send emails, a few letters and in some parts of the world people still send faxes. Regardless of what form the writing takes and how it's sent, there are common phrases which are used in day-to-day business correspondence. The selection of those phrases listed below have a neutral business register; in other words, they are neither very formal nor too informal and so are appropriate to many different contexts.

You'll also find a photocopiable activity on p165 which provides practice with email phrases. Make copies of the phrase for each pair or small group of students. Cut them up and students place them randomly on the table. Tell your students to match the phrases with the same meaning and put the more formal expression on the left and less formal on the right. Students can also play pelmanism with them by turning them all face down on the table. One student turns two over. If they are the matching expressions, they keep them and go again. If not, the next player turns two over until all the pairs of expressions have been found.

1. Starting

Dear Sir or Madam / Mr. Smith / Ms Waters / Mrs Kiralti

Hi Joan / Hello Robert

2. Reasons for writing and replying

I'm writing to …/ With regard to …

Further to your request for…

In reply to your email/letter about …

3. A friendly response

Thank you for your email.

Nice/Great to hear from you again.

I'm glad everything is going well.

4. Request

I'm writing to ask you for …

I would be grateful if you …

Please could you …?

Can I ask you to …?

5. Good news

We're delighted to inform you that …

I have some good news about …

6. Bad news

I'm writing with some bad news about …

I'm sorry/regret to inform/tell you that …

Unfortunately …

7. Apologise

Please accept our sincere apologies …

I'm afraid that …

I'd like to apologise for …

8. Attachments (and enclosures)

Please find attached/enclosed …

I'm attaching/enclosing …

I've also attached/enclosed a copy of …

9. Future contact

If you have any further questions, do not hesitate to email me.

Feel free to contact me on …

I look forward to hearing from you.

See you soon.

10. Ending

Yours sincerely (UK) / Sincerely (US)

Best/Kind regards

Best wishes

"While social media has resulted in a wider variety of electronic written communication, email remains a key e-genre in the business world. Many learners, even those at higher levels, say that one of the things they struggle with most in writing business emails is gauging the correct style. They're often unsure of how formal or informal they should be. As a result, in lessons with them, I focus on example email messages with reasonably neutral language and highlight this. I point out that this language is appropriate for a variety of business contexts."

Craig Thaine, Teacher, Teacher Trainer & Materials Writer, Languages International, Auckland, New Zealand

10 business writing sub-skills

Unit 45

As well as identifying the types of writing texts students might have to produce (see Unit 43), there are various writing sub-skills that will improve students' all-round writing skills.

1. Titles, references and subject lines

Many different types of business documents require use of titles, headings and sub-headings (in reports), reference lines (in letters) and subject lines (in emails or memos). So students need to be able to look at a text and decide what the key words are and turn these into a short heading. One way to approach this in class is to gather together a collection of short emails (or make some up) and remove the subject lines. Students can work on their own or in pairs and try to come up with the subject lines. At the end, they compare their versions with the originals. You can also vary the task by putting a word limit on the subject lines, e.g. no more than three words.

2. Register and formality

Students find it hard to recognise the level of formality in writing and to produce it themselves. You could take one text and rewrite it either more formally or less formally and ask students which is the more formal. They could also list the reasons why. Another useful exercise is to take different phrases (see Unit 44) and have them try to match phrases with the same meaning but decide which is more formal. For example, here's an extract from such an exercise:

1. *Dear Mr Thorn*
2. *Thank for your letter which arrived yesterday.*
3. *I'd be delighted to join you next week.*

A. *Great to hear from you again.*
B. *Hi Geoff*
C. *It'd be great to see you next week.*

(Answers: 1b, 2a, 3c. 1-3 are more formal)

3. Numbering and bullet points

The ability to shorten a long text and turn it into a more manageable list of information is a useful skill, especially for people writing short reports or slides for a presentation. To practise, give students long texts and ask them to turn it into a list of numbered points.

4. Linkers and connectors

The types of linking and connecting words that students need to use is affected by their level. At lower levels they may use *and, but, so, or,* whereas at higher levels they start to make use of *in addition, nevertheless, however.* For controlled practice, give students pairs of sentences and they join them using the word in brackets. Here are some examples:

1. *The company was set up in 1999. At first it produced specialist parts of cars. (and)*
2. *By 2005 the company had doubled in size. Two years later, it's core market collapsed. (however)*
3. *To survive it expanded the business into mainstream car parts. It started servicing cars. (In addition)*

To make the task harder, remove the linkers in brackets and students have to decide what to use.

5. Cause and effect language

Cause and effect language includes verbs such as *causes, results in, leads to* and prepositional phrases like *as a result of, because of, due to*. Students who have to write processes will need to use this kind of language. For more ideas see Unit 26, activity 6.

6. Paragraphs and structure

For longer texts which include a number of paragraphs and a well-defined structure, try to find some examples and cut them into sections. Have students read the sections and try to piece them back together in a logical order. It's a useful way to draw attention to this feature of written texts.

7. Distancing language

A high level skill is making the style of language more or less impersonal. For example, you can use passive structures to make a report on a meeting more impersonal. Here is an extract from a longer exercise in which students have to rewrite the first sentence to make the second more formal and impersonal:

1. The board recommends that Mr Brown should resign from his post.

It was..

2. We have decided to end production at this plant.

It has..

3. We'll pay him a redundancy fee.

A redundancy fee...

(Answers: 1. It was recommended that Mr Brown should resign from his post. 2. It has been decided to end production at this plant. 3. A redundancy fee will be paid to him.)

Having done this, students should notice any more examples of this style of language in documents that they work with.

8. Elision

When teaching students to write short messages, it's helpful to give them examples first and ask them to notice what types of words are missing. For example, in this message 'See you at 8.' the subject 'I', the verb 'will', and the time reference 'in the morning' or in the evening' is missing. You can ask students to write short messages like this out in full. So if you wrote *'Can dept meet Tuesday?'* on the board, students would have to rewrite it as *'Can the department meet on Tuesday?'* You can also reverse the exercise by giving full sentences and students try to shorten them by leaving out words like the subject, articles, determiners and prepositions.

9. Abbreviations

Business and technical documents often include abbreviations. To start students off you can give them the most common ones such as *asap, Re., NB, encs, dept., FYI, btw, tbc, Dr.* Ask them to write them out in full (e.g. *as soon as possible, reference/regarding, nota bene, enclosures, department, for your information, by the way, to be confirmed, Doctor*) or make it a team quiz where they have to guess the meaning. Once they've done this, bring in authentic documents and ask them to search and note down any abbreviations they find. As a productive task, ask them to write short messages to each other using some of the abbreviations they find and see if their partner can decode the message afterwards.

10. Fluency

We often talk about being accurate when writing and it's very true that this is important in business writing. Your students will want you to read and correct their written work. But as in speaking, there is also such a thing as allowing time in class for students to become more fluent writers. This means writing at speed and often in response to other pieces of writing. You can provide practice with writing fluency by giving students a pairwork activity in which they have send messages/emails back and forth to each other in a short space of time. For example, write the following on the board and students have to write messages back and forth:

Student A: Invite B to a meeting today.

Student B: Explain you are too busy.

Student A: Suggest a different time.

Student B: Agree but ask for another day.

Student A: Agree.

Student B: Confirm the meeting.

In total, students will send eight different messages. These could take the form of emails or short text messages. Set a time limit of five minutes to complete the task. That way, they focus on fluency. As a follow-up task, ask them to read the eight messages again and check for accuracy.

"Sometimes it's difficult to get in-work students doing writing work in class. One thing that does work though is if they bring in examples of real written correspondence or short reports and you use this as a springboard."

Paul Dummett, Business English trainer and author

In Section 2 on preparation and planning (p25), we said that authentic materials in English are a key part of analysing a student's needs as they tell us so much about the type of English they deal with and their key areas of business. In the next two units we look at how to make use of authentic materials in your teaching. You might use them for supplementing your coursebook or you could build a whole course around them. Here are 10 useful types of authentic materials with tips on how they might be used, but be aware that you will often come across other items that can be integrated into your lessons, especially if you teach on site. The first seven relate specifically to authentic materials that you might find in a company which you can re-use in lessons for that company. The last three are authentic materials which are in the public domain and can be adapted for most lessons.

1. Company websites

Going online and reading the company's website must be the fastest way to learn what the company does and how it operates. In fact, the larger the company, the more sophisticated the website usually is. Website content ranges from a basic written description of the business through to interactive animations showing the production process. Without doubt, it is your starting point when working with a company. You can cut and paste text and images and turn them into language exercises for your students or write quizzes and see how much your students know about their own company. If they don't know the answer, tell them to go and find out from the (English versions of) the website.

2. An annual report

Larger public limited companies have to publish a report every year that must include three key financial statements: the balance sheet, the profit and loss account, and a cashflow statement. This makes them a good resource for students who need the English to talk about topics such as assets and liabilities. For example, if you have anyone from the finance department in your class, get them to give a presentation of the key information in the annual report.

3. The company newsletter

Despite the speed at which you get news about a company online, many businesses still publish a newsletter about their business, and often in English or its bilingual. You'll sometimes find it in the reception areas of a company where visitors wait and obviously it always presents a very positive picture of the company. There will be photographs of staff who have raised money for charity or details of the latest venture into a new market. It is a nice resource to bring into class and use to teach vocabulary to develop reading skills with comprehension questions.

4. Company videos

Find out if any of the companies you work with produce videos. These might include marketing and promotional videos, interviews with the CEO or even documentaries about their production processes. They offer a great opportunity for listening practise but you could also turn the sound off and have students add their own narration.

ETpedia: 500 ideas for Business English teachers © Pavilion Publishing and Media Ltd and its licensors 2016.

Unit 46

5. Your student's correspondence

As we saw in Unit 43 on business writing, the best way to know what kind of writing to teach your students is to see examples of what emails and correspondence they send and receive. In addition, these kinds of texts can also provide the basis for lessons with other students working in the same company as they will often contain subject matter relating to other employees' work. Obviously such material, which was written for personal use, needs to be handled appropriately. Ask a student for permission to re-use it with other classes and replace names and contact details with fictional names. You may have to rewrite certain sentences but you can normally keep the core vocabulary in the text. With this kind of material it's quick and easy to create gapfill exercises that provide targeted practice for your students.

6. Recordings

Another way to source authentic materials is to make your own. A particularly useful tool is a good audio recording device. This might be the app on your phone or, if possible, use a digital audio voice recorder which has good sound quality. You can interview different people or record a real presentation by someone in the company. Of course, if you intend to run these into listening comprehensions make sure you have the permission of people involved and that they understand how you intend to use their voices.

7. Notices

In companies where English is the official company language you'll often see notices on walls written in English. These might be warnings about certain machinery in a factory which are useful for using with technicians and factory floor workers or they might contain more general information.

8. Business news

Many newspapers have regular business news supplements or there are newspapers dedicated to the world of business such as the *Financial Times* or *The Economist*. Although they will be mainly of interest to students who are involved in the world of finance and investment they can offer excellent potential for reading lessons. For example, you can choose a variety of articles, remove the headlines and students have to match them, or ask students to create new headlines and then compare them with originals.

9. Business magazines

Unlike newspapers, business magazines tend to deal with the softer side of business. Quite often you'll find how-to type articles on topics like how to deal with other cultures when travelling or doing business with them, how to improve your communication skills or how to lead a team. These kinds of themes can provide good reading and talking points for lessons with many different students. One example of such a magazine is *Business Life* published by British Airways. It's provided on flights, but you can also subscribe to it or visit its website which re-publishes many of the texts.

10. Infographics and kinetic typography videos

In recent years a new text type has emerged that combines visual elements with language. They are called 'infographics' and a whole range of them have been created online on different topics. Many are related to the world of work so if you are looking for a text on a specific topic you will often find a related infographic. The design is often quite striking so they make useful short reading texts to use in class. As a follow-up activity, students can even create their own infographics using a web tool like Piktochart. Another variation of the infographic text is the kinetic typography video. This is a video which combines animated text and images. You can search for these online by typing in a business word + kinetic typography. One simple activity to do with these is to give students some or all of the numbers and figures which appear in the video. They then have to watch and note down what the figures refer to. It's a particularly challenging but fun reading task.

"Students can sometimes feel that they do not perform to the best of their ability as they are not familiar with a topic. Infographics can be a useful, quick and efficient way to build knowledge on common areas. Using infographics can help students feel confident and secure in a range of topic areas."

Louis Rogers, teacher and author

Read more about speaking skills in a post by Louis at www.myetepdia.com

Once you have authentic materials you will want to use them in different ways during your lesson. Most of the exercises below will lend themselves to working with reading texts and some of them will also work with recorded listenings or videos.

1. Leading in with pictures

If the authentic materials include pictures such as photographs or diagrams, it's always worth starting some classroom discussion about these before the students do any reading (or listening). Ask questions such as *What does it show? Where do you think it is? What do you think the reading/listening is going to be about?*

2. Comprehension questions

With any reading or listening text the obvious starting point is to write comprehension questions to direct the students reading and to check they understand the text. Typically these might be open comprehension questions that require one word answers such as *'What does the company produce?' 'How many people work in its headquarters?'*

3. True/false sentences

Instead of writing questions, you could offer sentences and ask students to decide if they are true or false according to the reading or listening text. For example:

1. The company produces bicycles. True / False
2. Over three hundred people work in the headquarters. True / False

4. Multiple-choice questions

Another variation to the basic comprehension question is to provide a choice of optional answers, like this:

1. The company produces …
a. bicycles   b. boats   c. different leisure transport

5. Remove sentences

With longer written texts, remove certain sentences and leave gaps in the text. Students read and try to decide where the missing sentences should go.

6. Match the words to the definitions

If you are using a text which contains lots of new vocabulary, you could write the definitions of these words and then students have to match the words in the text to the correct definitions. They could use dictionaries to help if necessary.

7. Gapfills

If you have been focusing on certain language points, you could try gapping words in the text for students to fill with target language. To make it easier, the words could be given separately for students to choose from or they could choose from three words, like this:

1.   Mr Brewster is in charge ___ our R&D division

a. in   b. of   c. for

With listening texts you can create similar questions so that students listen and tick the word they hear.

8. Summarising a text

With either a reading or listening text, it can be useful for students to try and summarise it into a short text. It makes them focus on understanding the key points and integrates their writing skills.

9. Dictating a text

Students can work in pairs and take turns to read parts of a text aloud. Their partner has to write down word for word what they hear.

10. A presentation

At the end of working with an authentic material such as an informational text, students can practise presentation skills by preparing a short presentation based on what they've read.

"Together with your students, choose authentic listening materials which reflect their interests and communication needs. Focus on the vocabulary, grammar and functional language which the speakers use in natural speech and help to sensitise your students to different accents and cultural contexts. Explore how some speakers express themselves clearly whilst others do not. Help your learners to develop active listening techniques for when they do not understand".

Ian Badger, communications trainer and author, Bristol, UK

10 types of test used on business English courses

On any kind of language course teachers give students tests for a number of different reasons. More formal tests might be a standard test of a student's level of English. Perhaps the head of training wants regular checks of students' progress, so you'll need to test students during the course. Or sometimes we use tests less formally in class simply as a motivational tool or even because our students expect to be tested. Here is an overview of the types of tests needed and tips on how you might design tests for different purposes.

1. Placement test

When you have large numbers of students who need to be grouped by level, then a placement test is a fast way to find this out. Placement tests can be purchased commercially or your school may already have such a test. Note that it doesn't have to have questions related to business as the aim is to find out their general level. You can also give placement tests at the beginning of a course for small groups or one-to-one simply as a way to assess their general level before going on to diagnose their individual strengths and weaknesses. Many placement tests and references to levels of English follow the CEFR levels. (See explanation of CEFR on p134.)

2. Diagnostic test

Like a placement test, a diagnostic test can be given at the beginning of a course as part of the needs analysis process, but unlike a placement test it is not designed to find out a general level. Instead it can be written to assess students' ability in particular areas. For example, if you know that your students need to be able to make telephone calls in English for their job, then you could design a test which diagnoses how effectively they can (or can't) complete certain tasks on the phone. You could interview each student and role play a telephone situation to find this information out.

3. Progress test

This kind of test is given at different stages of the course to check if students have learned the content of the course. If you are using a Business English course book then many provide progress tests to give after each unit. Alternatively, when you design your own test, make sure you are only testing what has been taught in your lessons so far.

4. Achievement test

This test is normally given at the end of a course or after a significant amount of time. It should provide a global score and indicate the level of progress that a student has made over the period of the course. Companies who are paying for their staff to attend will be very interested in the results from such a test.

5. Speaking tests

If you want to test speaking skills in particular then the best way is to have a one-to-one situation with you interviewing a student. You can ask general questions as well as questions about business topics. Remember to get the student to ask you questions as well. You could also ask the student to prepare a short presentation beforehand and follow up with questions. If you know the student has to attend meetings or make phone calls, then choose a role play situation and simulate the conversation with the student. If you are testing a large number of students then you can also interview two students at the same time. Make sure you give each student equal opportunity to speak and make use of the fact that there are two of them by asking them to role play a situation in which they talk to each other and you sit back and listen. To help grade their performances it might also be worth recording the interviews. This also helps if anyone queries your assessment and you need to provide evidence.

6. Listening tests

There are many commercially produced listening materials that you could use to form the basis for a listening test. You could make your own, but you will have to ensure that the sound quality is good enough for test conditions. Another possibility is to read a text aloud (e.g. a presentation) and set students questions on the content. Where possible, design the listening activity so that it reflects a real business task, such as making notes in a presentation or writing details down from a voicemail message.

7. Reading tests

If you are testing students' general reading skills (e.g. for a placement test) then choose texts which don't require specialised knowledge of a specific business area otherwise you might be testing subject expertise rather than the level of English. For a progress test, select texts which resemble the same types of texts used in class and that include vocabulary taught so far.

8. Writing tests

To assess general level, set a broad writing topic such as 'Describe your job and the company you work for'. For diagnostic or progress tests you will want to include writing tasks that reflect course content and the types of writing that students deal with in their day-to-day work. For example, if you want to test email writing you could give students an email from a fictional client and ask them to write a reply.

9. Multiple choice tests

Many placement tests and also some achievement tests take the form of giving students sentences with gaps in. Usually, students are given a selection of A, B,C, D answers to choose from. This kind of test can establish a student's global level, although it's less effective as a diagnostic test for particular business skills. If you want to test grammar, vocabulary or fixed expressions used in business communication, then this kind of test can be reasonably precise, not to mention quick and easy to administer (and mark).

10. Quick classroom tests

Teachers can use tests at any time of the lesson to check students' progress. One popular form is the 'Ticket out the door test' which means you assess whether students can recall a certain number of new language items from the lesson. Another quick test could be one at the beginning of the lesson with the teacher checking if students remember key vocabulary from the previous lesson. These kinds of tests don't have to take long to prepare. They might be eight words gapped in a paragraph or you could dictate a text with target language in and see if students can write out the complete text. (See Unit 41.)

Students – even adult business students – can find this kind of testing motivating and enjoy the opportunity to test themselves. As an extension, put students into teams and have them prepare tests for another team by looking back through their classroom materials and selecting new language to test. It can get competitive, fun and is very useful.

Common European Framework Levels

In 1990, an organisation was formed called the Association of Language Teachers in Europe (ALTE). One of its main aims was to develop a system in Europe which allowed language certificates issued in different countries to be recognised across borders. One result of ALTE's work was a series of 'can do' statements that were listed under the level headings of A1, A2, B1, B2, C1 and C2.

Since their creation, the 'Common European Framework Levels' have become widely-known in other continents as well as in Europe, and you will often see the levels printed on the covers of coursebooks or referred to in literature about levels and testing.

Here's an overview of how the CEFR levels relate to general level descriptors:

A1: Beginner, False beginner, Elementary

A2: Elementary, Pre-intermediate

B1: Low-intermediate, Intermediate

B2: Intermediate, Upper-intermediate

C1: Advanced

C2: Proficient

In the previous unit we looked at the type of tests you can produce for your Business English classes and how you might write them. However, some students might want to take a formally recognised qualification at the end of their course or their companies might require it. Here is a list of some of the best-known examinations aimed at Business English learners. Visit the website for full details and to find out if the exam is available in your region.

1. Business English Certificates (BEC)

Cambridge English is a well-known examinations board with many general English exams every year. Its Business English Certificates are popular with students and companies because the three levels of exam test speaking, reading, writing and listening. Each level corresponds to a CEFR level making it a useful benchmark for employers. The three levels are:

▶ BEC Preliminary (CEFR B1)

▶ BEC Vantage (CEFR B2)

▶ BEC Higher (CEFR C1)

www.cambridgeenglish.org/exams/business-certificates

2. BULATS (Business Language Testing Service)

The BULATS test is also offered by Cambridge English but unlike its BEC qualifications, the test can only be taken online and it's an assessment of a student's current level. You can get an immediate result and report on the student's level making it very useful for placing student by level and for checking if a new recruit has the English level needed.

www.bulats.org

3. LCCI English for Business

The LCCI (London Chamber of Commerce and Industry) offers a variety of examinations in different areas of business (including accountancy and tourism) but their English for Business exams at four different levels are probably the most popular for students needing a Business English qualification. There is a compulsory reading and writing paper and an optional speaking and listening component.

http://qualifications.pearson.com/en/qualifications/lcci.html

4. LCCI Spoken English for Industry and Commerce

For students needing to take a test of speaking only, then the LCCI exam known as SEFIC will test them at five different levels. The exam takes the format of a one-to-one interview with an official examiner. Students have to talk about a variety of business topics and deal with a range of situations depending on their level.

http://qualifications.pearson.com/en/qualifications/lcci.html

Unit 49

5. TOEIC

The Test of English for International Communication or TOEIC exam tests all four skills with an emphasis on real-life work situations. As a result, it's often used by companies to test employee's English when planning their staffing requirements. Candidates receive a final score between 10 and 990 points.

https://www.ets.org/toeic

6. IELTS

The International English Language Testing System, better known as IELTS, is not aimed specifically at business learners but many in-work students or students interested in furthering their careers may ask you to help prepare them for it. The exam tests the four skills and the content is a mixture of general topics and more academic ones. It's internationally recognised and many students take it to enter universities in other countries or even to gain a visa. When recruiting, many companies will accept an IELTS score as useful evidence of a candidate's language level.

http://www.ielts.org/about_us.aspx

7. Spoken English for Work (SEW)

Trinity exam board offers a number of different English exams and its Spoken English for Work is a useful test of spoken communication skills in a work context. It can test levels at CEFR B1, B2, B2+ and C1. The candidate is interviewed by an examiner and the tasks include a discussion, a presentation and a telephone call.

www.trinitycollege.com/sew

8. Cambridge General English Exams

BEC and BULATS in 1 and 2 are from Cambridge English which is an exam board better known for its general English exams such as First (FCE) and Advanced (CAE). Some in-work students may choose these exams because they are more widely known and some companies ask for them.

http://www.cambridgeenglish.org/exams/academic-and-professional-english/

9. TOEFL

The Test of English as a Foreign Language or TOEFL is from ETS who also produce the TOEIC exam (see 5). TOEFL tests the four skills and is taken by learners aiming to enter university but also for workers applying for overseas visas. As a result, your students might request preparation for TOEFL instead of TOEIC.

http://www.ets.org/toefl

10. Pearson Test of English

This computer-based exam is available to test general or academic English. A score on the PTE (Academic) is accepted by many leading business universities so students planning to study business at graduate and post-graduate level may ask you to prepare them for this exam.

http://www.pearsonvue.com/pte/

10 ways to go on developing your Business English teaching skills

As you teach more and more Business English you'll probably decide to develop your skills further. This might take the form of completing a course and gaining more qualifications, but professional development comes in many forms. Here are 10 suggestions.

1. Variety

Probably the most effective way to develop your Business English teaching skills is to keep teaching students from different business backgrounds with different needs. So one day you might be teaching an environmental officer at a car factory who needs to write reports in English and the next you could be working with a group of 10 sales reps who need great presentation skills. You'll learn so much about different aspects of business from these people that it'll make you an even more effective teacher.

2. Share

Many Business English teachers find that they often work in different companies and don't come into contact with other teachers as much as they would in a language school. It's important that you find ways to meet other teachers from time to time and share your experiences and ideas. If you're lucky this might take the form of a workshop among a group of teachers but even an informal chat in a coffee bar with a couple of other teachers can be highly productive.

3. Business English coursebooks

For many Business English teachers, their initial main support will often come from using a comprehensive course book published for Business English courses. These books normally provide enough materials for a year-long course or you can pick and choose the parts that are relevant to your students' needs. In addition, many of these books also include additional teacher's editions with answer keys, progress tests and extra activities, as well as online support. Among the best-known titles are *Business Result* (Oxford), *Market Leader* (Pearson), *In-company* (Macmillan), and *Business Advantage* (Cambridge). For BEC preparation courses (Unit 49), there's *Success with BEC* (Summertown/Cengage Learning). Many of the publishers also have shorter books aimed at specialist courses in communication skills or for different industries such as energy, fashion or tourism. Using books like this is especially helpful for new teachers as they give you a ready-made course structure, but by using them you'll also get a useful grounding in all the different aspects of Business English.

4. Webinars

Many of the publishers who produce the coursebooks mentioned above also offer free webinars on a variety of topics including Business English. They might mention their products but in general the webinars tend to be neutral and aimed at any kind of teacher. They are a great way to receive training and development. In particular, Oxford and Macmillan offer regular webinars connected to Business English topics.

Unit 50

5. BESIG

BESIG is the Business English Special Interest Group of the much larger teacher's organisation, IATEFL. It has conferences and workshops in Europe although its regular online webinars are open to members from all over the world. It's an excellent group for learning about what's new in Business English and for networking with like-minded teachers. Visit besig.org for more details.

6. Teaching qualifications

There is no one route in Business English teaching. Many teachers come via a general English background at first, perhaps having taken a TKT, CELTA or Cert TESOL qualification. Some other teachers have experience of the business world before moving into teaching the language needed to talk about it. If you are interested in gaining a specific qualification, there is the Certificate in International Business English Training. For a list of providers and more details visit english.co.uk or trinitycollege.com. The LCCI offer a written exam leading to the First Certificate in Teaching Business English qualification. Another option is to take a DELTA, Diploma in TESOL or even an MA in ELT. Some MAs will include the opportunity to research in different areas so you could develop your interest in Business English via this route.

7. Business qualifications

If you feel well-qualified in teaching, then you might want to look into developing your own business knowledge. Find out if a local college offers any short courses in management and professional skills. Often these are designed for people who are sent along by their employer but there's no reason why you shouldn't join such courses. They can be extremely helpful in giving background in topics such as management and leadership, selling skills, online marketing and so on.

8. Business books

Books about business fill many shelves in larger bookshops. They cover a range of topics which will bring you up to date on the latest trends in the business world or include ideas and theories by well-known business people such as Tom Peters, Richard Branson or Bill Gates. These types of books give you a crash course in business theory and will make useful reference titles later on.

9. Business news and magazines

Publications such as the *Financial Times, The Economist, Fast Company, Inc., Management Today,* and *Forbes* magazines are just some of the main newspapers and magazines aimed at business readers. As we saw in Units 46 and 47 they can be useful as authentic materials to bring into the classroom but they are also an excellent way of developing your own business knowledge. All the major titles also have websites giving access to many past articles.

Unit 50

10. Materials writing, blogging and self-publishing

As you become more experienced you will probably start to write more and more of your own materials. These might be based on authentic materials your students give you (see Unit 46) or you might start to develop content that other teachers can use. You might try posting some of these materials online. You could start your own blog (using wordpress.com) or some Business English teachers are self-publishing (using sites like smashwords.com). Other Business English teachers also offer online materials directly aimed at their learners. Writing and publishing offers you a chance to let others test out your materials as well as adding a new strand to your Business English career.

> *"If you are serious about your professional development as a Business English teacher/ trainer, you definitely need to be a member of IATEFL-BESIG (www.besig.org), take part in its conferences, webinars and online weekend workshops, and read its regular publication* Business Issues. *Also, get involved in the BESIG-community, contribute to its publication and apply to present at its events. Many publishers also offer webinars and events that are relevant to business English. "*
>
> **Ian McMaster, Editor-in-chief of the magazine *Business Spotlight*, Munich, Germany**

Unit 50

10 more activities for Business English teaching from the original ETpedia

The first ever *ETpedia* resource book for English language teachers was published in 2014. With over 1,000 ideas for teachers and presented in the accessible style of 10 tips, activities or ideas per unit, it provides support to teachers in every area of ELT, including Business English teachers. To support your teaching, here's a selection of 10 ideas, tips and activities from the original *ETpedia* which will be useful in your Business English classroom. And don't forget to visit www.myetpedia.com where you'll find more ideas for teachers on the blog as well as full details about the *ETpedia* resource books.

1. A first day of the course activity with photos (from Unit 9.6)

Bring in some photographs of yourself, your family and friends. Show them round the class and talk about them or invite questions about the pictures. Extend the activity by asking your students to bring photographs of themselves to the lesson and to talk about them in a similar way. Alternatively, if your students are allowed to use their mobile phones in class, they could show photographs to each other on their phones and talk about them.

2. A listening exercise where students test their partner (from Unit 39.8)

You can write comprehension questions to get the students to listen for specific information or you can ask them to write their own. Give each student a copy of the script for the listening. (Usually published course materials include copies of these scripts.) Ask them to write five comprehension questions which will require someone to listen in order to find the answers. Then take away the scripts and ask the students to swap their questions with a partner. Play the listening and the students try to answer their partner's comprehension questions.

3. Travel problems (from Unit 21.2)

Travel and holidays are something that most students have experience of, so there are different ways to lead into a lesson on this topic. The subject of travel problems is especially good because it usually prompts some interesting travel anecdotes from well-travelled students. Write the following on the board and ask the students if they have ever had any problems with them: *delays and cancellations – car hire – being stopped at customs – the local food – a hotel room – illness – missed trains or flights – passports and visas – the local language – a taxi driver – other*. If a student says they have, then ask them to tell the class what happened.

4. Telephoning with voicemail dictation (from Unit 41.10)

Explain to your students that they will leave a message on a voicemail for a friend asking him or her to meet tonight. Ask the class what type of information they will need to give. For example, *the time and date of the call, the time/date they want to meet, the name of the location to meet, what they want to do.* They will also need to spell any difficult words (such as names) and clarify the numbers in the dates or times. When each student has written their message, they take turns in pairs to dictate their message as if recording a voicemail. Their partner listens and writes down the key information.

5. Brainstorming in groups using the *'Yes and ...'* technique (from Unit 32.4)

This idea comes from the main idea behind improvisation in drama; the idea being that when someone adds something new or makes a suggestion, it is never judged but always welcomed. The same principle can be applied to brainstorming business ideas in the language classroom. Choose a situation in which students will need to brainstorm ideas. For example, you could put the students in groups of three or four and tell them that they all work for the same company. Their company produces one type of 'pen' (or any object). However, in order to remain competitive, the company needs to create some new types of pens. The group has three to five minutes to brainstorm as many different types of pen as possible. One person starts the discussion with the words 'I think we should create a new type of pen.' From then on, any of the students can speak but they must start every sentence with the words 'Yes and...'. This forces them to suggest a new idea for a pen every time they speak. In this way, the group generate lots of new ideas. Stop them after five minutes and ask them review and note down all the ideas they had. Then they have to summarise the features of their new pen and present it to the rest of the class.

6. Problem-solving skills by creating a mouse trap (Unit 27.10)

This problem-solving activity is creative, good for teamwork and often appeals to any technician or engineers in the class. Write a list of random objects on the board such as *a long piece of string, glue, a car tyre, a pulley, a tennis racquet, an elephant, a pen.* You can even ask students to suggest one or two other objects to add to the list. Overall, you need between about seven and nine. Put students into discussion groups of four. Each group needs a large blank sheet of paper (A3 size or bigger if possible) and marker pens. Explain that the group works together in an office and they have seen a mouse. Using only the objects listed on the board, they must discuss, design and draw a way to capture the mouse. The rule is that they must use ALL the objects and nothing extra. Allow about twenty minutes for the groups to create their mouse traps and then ask each group to show their design and present it.

ETpedia™
1,000 ideas for English language teachers

7. Writing instructions for a paper plane (from Unit 52.3)

Give a piece of blank paper to students in groups of three or four. Ask them to make a paper plane. This task generates useful speaking and discussion as they try to agree and decide on a design. Once everyone has made their plane (and tested it), tell them to try to write a set of instructions to give to another group so they can make the same plane. Encourage them to use instructional language, such as imperative verb forms and sequencing words like *Firstly*, *Secondly*, etc. When they have written their instructions, they swap them with another group and try to reproduce the other group's plane. At the end, everyone compares their paper planes and comments on how clear (or unclear) the instructions were.

8. An invited classroom guest (from Unit 38.9)

Invite an outside business speaker to come to the lesson and give a presentation. This is a good way for your students to be exposed to other types of accents and different ways of speaking. If the speaker is prepared to take questions from the class as well, then the listening activity has a real sense of purpose to it. For such a situation, students could prepare their questions in advance.

9. An imaginary visitor (from Unit 87.9)

When teaching one-to-one you can bring a 'third' person to a lesson by having a picture of someone or a prop like a hat. When you pick up the picture or prop you become a different person. This allows you to have a three-way discussion with the student if necessary.

10. At the end of a lesson use 'Can-do' statements (from Unit 14.4)

There is a trend in ELT nowadays to define language learning in terms of 'can do' statements. For example, we can define a language objective with a statement like 'I can order food in a restaurant'. You might have a course syllabus written this way or course materials sometimes include 'can-do' statements at the end of a page for the students to review their learning. However, it's easy enough to adapt this idea so that students complete sentences starting with the words 'I can…' and they write what they can now do in English as a result of the lesson.

To see sample pages or to buy now – go to www.etprofessional.com
Email: **info@etprofessional**   Call our orders hotline: **+44 (0)1273 434 943**

Price: £28.95

Order code: E166

ISBN: 978-1-910366-13-4

Appendix

Needs analysis form

Name: ....

Company: ....

Job title: ....

Describe your main responsibilities: ....

English in your work

Who do you regularly communicate with in English?

What do you communicate about?

How do you usually communicate in English? (By phone, by email, in meetings?)

Learning English

Have you studied English before?

Do you have any qualifications in English?

How much time do you have for studying after the lessons?

Your course

Which of these areas of English do you think you need to improve on this course? Write a number from 1 to 3 (3 = very important for me, 2 = important, 1 = not important for me).

General vocabulary		Meetings and discussions	
Grammar		Giving presentations	
Pronunciation		Negotating	
Reading		Listening	
Writing		Vocabulary for my job	
Speaking		Social English	
Reading and writing business correspondence			
Reading and writing business documents			

What else would you like to learn on your course?

Do you have any questions about the course?

Student A

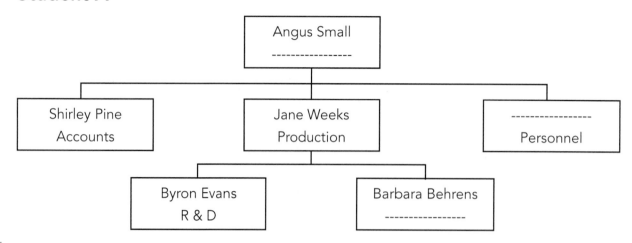

- Cut along this line ✂ -

Student B

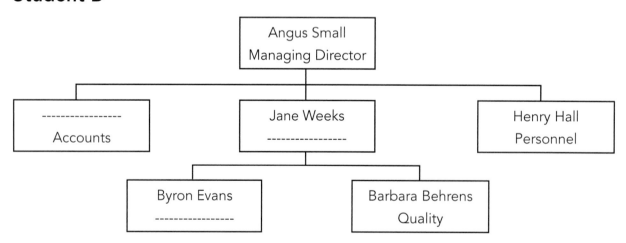

Directions in a company

Student A

	General manager	Marketing	

	Entrance and reception	

IT and maintenance		Cafeteria	

- Cut along this line ✂ -

Student B

Conference room	General manager		

Customer service and call centre		Car park

	Toilets	

Appendix

Collocation pelmanism

market	research	advertising	campaign
product	launch	free	sample
end	user	marketing	director
market	share	press	release
advertising	hoarding	target	market
brand	stretching	customer	feedback
mail	shot	special	offer

Scoresheet for elevator pitch

As you watch the elevator pitch, score each aspect of the pitch with a score from 0 (poor) to 4 (very good).

	0	1	2	3	4
Opening (How well does the speaker get your attention?)					
Clarity (Is the message clear?)					
Interest (Is the pitch interesting? Do you want to hear more?)					
Pace (Is it the right speed? Not too slow and not too fast.)					
Timing (Is it the right length?)					
Communication (Is the language natural and effective?)					
Conclusion (Does it end well? Is it clear what the speaker wants?)					
Total					

Appendix

Communicative crossword

Student A

- Cut along this line ✂ -

Student B

Finance quiz

1   Where is this coin from?

2   What is the currency of Thailand?

3   When was the euro launched?

4   How do you pronounce this word – *debt?*

5   Who painted the most expensive painting ever sold at auction?

6   Complete this title. _____ *can't buy me love.*

7   Make a word from these letters: LLMNRIIEOAI.

8   Complete this title. *The Wolf of* _____

9   Where is Fort Knox?

10 If you tighten your _____ you will spend less money.

- Cut along this line ✂ -

Answers:

1 Great Britain, 2 Thai Bhat, 3 1st January, 1999, 4 /det/, 5 Picasso (for $179 million), 6 Money, 7 millionaire, 8 Wall Street, 9 The state of Kentucky, USA, 10 belt.

151

Describing trends on graphs

Draw a trend line on this graph for a company's turnover. Then describe it to your partner who will try to draw it. For example: *In 2005, the company turnover was 1.5 million. Then, in 2006 it rose by another half a million and in 2007 it stayed the same....*

Turnover

	2005	2006	2007	2008	2009	2010	2011	2012	2013	2014	2015
5m											
4.5m											
4m											
3.5m											
3m											
2.5m											
2m											
1.5m											
1m											

- Cut along this line ✂ -

GRAPH 2

Listen to your partner's description and draw the trend line on this graph.

Turnover

	2005	2006	2007	2008	2009	2010	2011	2012	2013	2014	2015
5m											
4.5m											
4m											
3.5m											
3m											
2.5m											
2m											
1.5m											
1m											

ETpedia: 500 ideas for Business English teachers © Pavilion Publishing and Media Ltd and its licensors 2016.

Staff benefits collocations

company	car	fringe	benefits
staff	discount	health	insurance
private	pension	annual	bonus
paid	holiday	language	training
gym	membership	subsidised	canteen
annual	medical	clothing	allowance

1. *My colleague never finishes his work on time and the manager always asks me to help him. I have to finish my work alone and then someone else's. And he is paid more!*

2. *I have been late three times this month and my manager has sent me a warning letter. The problem is I have three children to get to school and no car to get here. The bus is often very slow.*

3. *I have a very noisy, messy colleague who sings to herself all day and eats sweets very loudly. Her desk is untidy and she must spend about an hour a day making tea. It's really annoying.*

4. *My manager never seems to have any ideas, but every time we make a suggestion she puts it into action. She has just been promoted but we have been told there is no pay-rise this year.*

5. *I think my colleague's partner works for a competitor.*
   She is really good at her job so it's a bit unfair to mention it.

6. *I can't see why they picked him. She was so much better and so much nicer. I am not sure I want to stay if he is the new manager.*

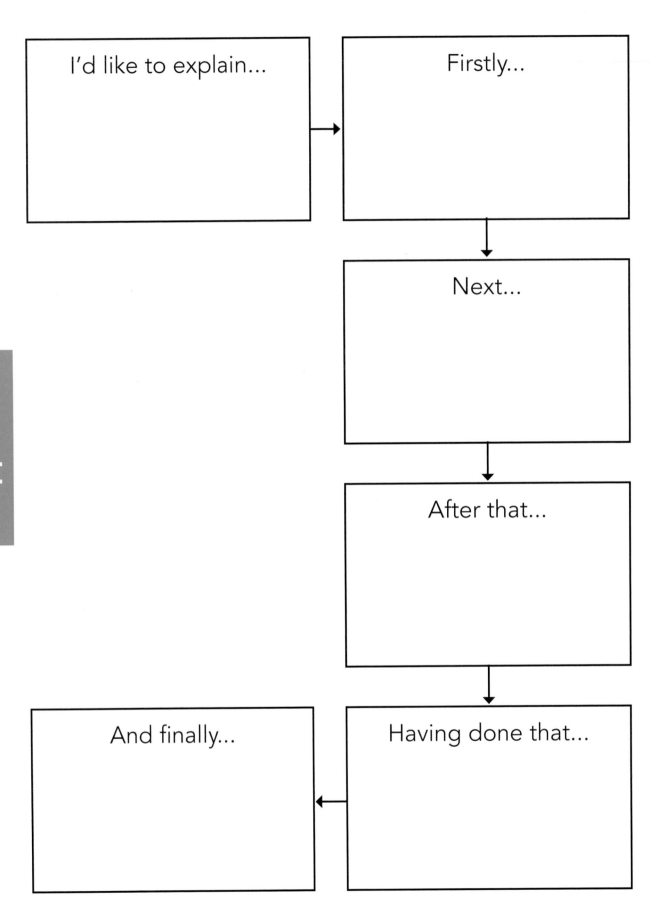

I'd like to explain...

Firstly...

Next...

After that...

And finally...

Having done that...

Appendix

Cut up script

Hi. My name's Jurgen Vettorel. Nice to meet you.

Nice to meet you too. I'm Lucia Marks. I'm with OIG.
Who do you work for?

I'm a consultant so I'm freelance.

That's interesting. What kind of areas do you work on?

Mainly management training. Team-building and so on.

That's a coincidence. I'm looking for someone to run courses
on that at the moment. Do you have a card?

Sure. Here you are. And I also have this brochure and my
website has more details.

Great. I'll take a look at it.

If you have some time now, we could get a coffee and I'll tell
you a bit more about what I do.

Actually, I must go to the next talk. But if you're around
later/afterwards, we could meet.

OK, let's meet again here in an hour.

See you then.

ETpedia: 500 ideas for Business English teachers © Pavilion Publishing and Media Ltd and its licensors 2016.

Tick the Social English phrase you use or hear

	Tick ✓		Tick ✓
Hello, my name's…		Great!	
Pleased/Nice to meet you.		Would you like a …?	
Nice to meet you, too.		Can I get you a drink?	
I'm in charge of …		Thanks, I'd like a …	
Who do you work for?		That's very kind of you. I'll have a …	
What do you do?		No thanks, I'm OK.	
Where are you from?		Let me introduce you to …	
How long have you been with …?		Have you met …?	
So have you been with [your company] a long time?		Do you know …?	
When did you start?		This is … . She's in charge of …	
Who were you with before that?		Here's my card.	
Have you always lived in …?		Do you have a card?	
Tell me more about …		What's your number?	
Have you ever worked for …?		Keep in touch.	
I studied … at university. What about you?		Give me a call next time you're in …	
Do you play much sport?		I'm afraid I have to go.	
That's interesting.		It was really nice meeting/talking to you.	
Really?		Maybe I'll see you again soon.	
I see.		I look forward to seeing you again.	
I didn't know that.		Goodbye.	

The Social English game

11 The person opposite you is a waiter. Order a meal in the restaurant.

10 You are at a local restaurant. Recommend a local dish to all the other players. Describe what is in the dish.

9 Invite all the other players to lunch at a restaurant.

8 Another person arrives at the meeting. Introduce the person on your left to the person on your right.

12 While eating, make small talk. Ask another player about their holiday plans next year.

7 Offer the person opposite you something to drink.

13 It's the end of the meal. Offer to pay the bill. Do the other players accept your offer?

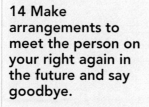

6 You are the Managing Director. Invite the person on your left into your office and ask about their journey.

14 Make arrangements to meet the person on your right again in the future and say goodbye.

5 You are waiting outside the office with the person on your right. Make small talk by asking him or her a question.

How to play:

1 Play the game in groups of four.

2 Put your counter on the START.

3 Roll a dice and move round the board.

4 Follow the instructions on the square and talk to another player.

5 To land on the FINISH square you must roll the correct number on the dice.

15 There are no taxis to the train station. Ask any other player about public transport to the train station.

4 The lift is out of order. Take the stairs and miss a go.

FINISH

START

1 You are visiting a company. Arrive and introduce yourself to the player on your left who works in reception.

2 You work in reception. Ask the player on your left about their job and company.

3 Ask the person on your right to give you directions to the Managing Director's office.

Maciej Bartosz

Bartosz Fashions

28 Warszawa Street, Radom, Poland

+48 610 8873   m.bart@bartosz.pl

Mina Khan

G.D. Regional Office
P.O Box 23425
Dubai, UAE

+97 149 284 465

m.khan@GDRO.com

Eduardo Urriola

Language & Translation specialist
4a Independence Square
Bogotá, Colombia
+57 4610 756

Enterprise
Office Rentals

Kristina Ultvedt

Munch Museum Street
Oslo, Norway
+47 657 3845
www.enterpriseoslo.org/about

Chris Astorina
Pisa Publishing

23 via Colombo
Milan, Italy
c.astorina@pisap.it
0039 45624190

Julie McCabe
Two Horse Travel

Alton Tower, 33 Moray St, New Farm, Brisbane
QLD 4005, Australia
+ 61 7 53240182
Email: jmccabe@bigpond.com

Atif Amari
ARB communications

22nd Floor,
Kingdom Tower
P.O. Box 50862
Riyadh

atif@arbriyadh.sa

Derrin Klausner
Prentis Exports & Logistics
Boston, USA
001 465 8394 2066
d.klausner@prentis.com

Cut up phrases for meetings and discussions

The purpose of the meeting is to …	The aim of this discussion is to …
What we want to do by the end of this meeting is to …	What do you think about …?
What's your opinion?	Do you agree with/ about …?
I think …	In my opinion …
It's my view that …	I agree.
You're absolutely right.	I think so too.
I disagree.	I don't agree.
I can't agree with you.	I agree with you up to a point but…

Turn the page for more phrases

A lot of what you are saying is true, but …	Yes, but …
Can I interrupt you there because …?	Before you continue I'd like to say that …
I'd like to say something …	But …
Please, let me finish …	Sorry but I'd like to finish …
Just one more thing and then you can speak …	So what you're saying is …?
Let me check I've understood you …	So if I've understood you correctly …
So let's sum up what we've discussed so far.	Can I just summarise what we've agreed?
We've agreed/decided that …	Let's move on to the next point.

Feedback form for a presentation

As you watch the presentation, score each aspect of the presentation by circling a number from 1 to 5. Give reasons for your answers beneath.

The introduction ☹ 1 2 3 4 5 ☺

Comments:

The main content ☹ 1 2 3 4 5 ☺

Comments:

Use of language overall ☹ 1 2 3 4 5 ☺

Comments:

Use of signpost language ☹ 1 2 3 4 5 ☺

Comments:

Rapport with audience ☹ 1 2 3 4 5 ☺

Comments:

Eye contact and body language ☹ 1 2 3 4 5 ☺

Comments:

Visual aids ☹ 1 2 3 4 5 ☺

Comments:

Delivery ☹ 1 2 3 4 5 ☺

Comments:

Conclusion ☹ 1 2 3 4 5 ☺

Comments:

Handling questions ☹ 1 2 3 4 5 ☺

Comments:

1 You work for a manufacturing company with the following conditions:

- ▶ Current salary for most employees working in production: $35,000 per year
- ▶ Weekly hours: 40 hours per week. (There is currently no overtime.)
- ▶ Breaks: 1 hour for lunch, 2 short breaks in the morning and afternoon.
- ▶ Basic holidays: 20 days per year. 25 days per year for employees working more than 10 years.

Company proposal: Currently, employees work from 6am until 2pm or 2pm until 10pm. The management would like to introduce a night shift from 10pm until 6am. Employees would be asked to work different shifts so they sometimes worked a night shift as well as the other two shifts. Note that the unions think that the new scheme should come with some added benefits and a pay rise, especially for those employees working nights.

2 Your teacher will ask you to be a member of the management team or the trade union team. Work with your team and plan your negotiating position. Make notes on what you can offer or accept with regard to:

- ▶ Salary?
- ▶ Hours (including overtime)?
- ▶ Breaks?
- ▶ Holidays?
- ▶ Other benefits?

3 When you are ready, meet the other team and discuss your initial proposals. Find out where you can agree and where you disagree.

4 After 15 minutes, take a break and discuss the current position with your team. Prepare the next stage of the negotiation.

5 Meet the other side again and continue the negotiation.
Try to reach an agreement.

6 At the end, write a summary of what was agreed in the negotiation.

Match the email expressions

Dear Ms J. Smith	Hi Joan
With regard to your request for a meeting …	Thanks for your email about a meeting.
I'm delighted to hear from you.	Great to hear from you!
I would be grateful if you would attend the interview on Monday 5th April.	Can you come to the interview next Monday?
I'm sorry to inform you that your application was not successful this time.	Unfortunately, we can't offer you the job.
Please find attached a copy of the report.	The report is attached.
If you have any further questions, do not hesitate to contact me.	Call me if you have any questions.
I look forward to hearing from you soon.	Speak soon.
Yours sincerely	Best wishes

ETpedia: 500 ideas for Business English teachers © Pavilion Publishing and Media Ltd and its licensors 2016.

Appendix

Comparing products

	Product 1	Product 2	Product 3
Product/ Model name			
Height			
Width			
Depth			
Weight			
Price			
Other features			

A Company profile

Student A

Complete the information about this company. Ask your partner questions.

Company name: XPO Logistics

Area of business: (2) _____

Types of business partners includes: Construction, food retail, chemicals, automotive, electronics, textiles

Number of customers: (4) _____

Number of employees: 84,000

Locations: Operates in (6) _____ countries with _____ locations

Annual revenue: €4,669 million

Website: (8) _____
(Information based on website 2014 figures)

- Cut along this line ✂ -

Student B

Complete the information about this company. Ask your partner questions.

Company name: (1) _____

Areas of business: Supply chain solutions, transportation and storage

Types of business partners includes: (3) _____

_____

Number of customers: Over 50,000

Number of employees: (5) _____

Locations: Operates in 32 countries with 1,469 locations

Annual revenue: (7) _____

Website: www.europe.xop.com
(Information based on website 2014 figures)

Word-building

When you learn a new word, find other forms of the same word and write them in the table below.

Verb	Adjective	Noun	+ Prefix	Other forms	Collocations
produce	productive	product production	unproductive	productively (adv) producer (person)	mass-production
inform	informative	information	uninformed	informant (person)	information technology

Word search

T	R	A	I	N	I	N	G	O	S
E	G	P	A	L	T	O	N	I	C
D	R	P	R	O	R	D	E	R	H
E	P	R	A	G	L	O	G	I	E
A	F	A	C	I	L	I	T	Y	D
D	U	I	A	S	C	T	E	N	U
L	I	S	R	T	R	A	A	U	L
I	F	A	E	I	R	L	M	D	E
N	O	L	E	C	P	A	C	E	G
E	E	R	R	S	O	R	I	E	S

Appendix

Find the following words:

career, appraisal, facility, logistics, team, training, deadline, order, schedule

- Cut along this line ✂ -

Answer:

T	R	A	I	N	I	N	G		S
							L		C
D			O	R	D	E	R		H
E				G			R		E
A	F	A	C	I	L	I	T	Y	D
D			I	A	S			E	U
L			T	R	S		A		L
I				A	E	I		M	E
N				C	E	L			
E				S	R				

Alphabet game

In this game you have to think of words beginning with a letter of the alphabet connected to different categories. See the first examples under 'P'.

Next, you have 3 minutes to think of a word beginning with the letter 'M'. You earn 1 point for a correct answer but 2 points if nobody else has the same word. The winner is the person or team with the most points and can choose the next letter. Then start again and think of more words.

Letter	P	M			
Jobs	police officer				
Department	purchasing				
Office object	printer				
Country	Peru				
Food	peas				
Financial word	pay				
Factory word	process				
*					
*					

* You or your teacher can add two new topics here. For example, 'Important words for my job'.

Word stress

When you learn a new word, check you can pronounce it with the correct word stress. Write it under the correct word stress in this table. If the stress is not in the table, write the new word and its stress in the third row.

O	O o	o O	O o o
sales	product (n)	produce (v)	conference

o O o	o O o o	o o O o	o o o O o
recruitment	machinery	expectation	communication

Appendix

Contrastive stress dominoes

No, the <u>meeting</u> is at three.	So, we sold nine <u>hundred</u>?	No, we sold nine <u>thousand</u>.	Is that <u>E</u> as in <u>E</u>gypt?	No, <u>I</u> as in <u>I</u>taly.	Is that thir<u>teen</u>?
No, <u>thirty</u>.	Is the <u>meeting</u> at three?	No, the <u>presentation</u> is at three.	So, we <u>sold</u> nine hundred?	No, we <u>bought</u> nine hundred.	Is that <u>I</u> as in <u>I</u>taly?
No, <u>A</u> as in <u>A</u>ustria.	Is that <u>thirty</u>?	No, <u>fifty</u>.	Is the <u>presentation</u> at three?	No, the <u>seminar</u> is at three.	So, <u>we</u> sold nine hundred?
No, <u>they</u> sold nine hundred.	Is that <u>A</u> as in <u>A</u>ustria?	No, <u>E</u> as in <u>E</u>gypt.	Is that <u>fifty</u>?	No, fif<u>teen</u>.	Is the <u>seminar</u> at three?
No, the <u>meeting</u> is at three.	So, we sold nine <u>hundred</u>?	No, we sold nine <u>thousand</u>.	Is that <u>E</u> as in <u>E</u>gypt?	No, <u>I</u> as in <u>I</u>taly.	Is that thir<u>teen</u>?
No, <u>thirty</u>.	Is the <u>meeting</u> at three?	No, the <u>presentation</u> is at three.	So, we <u>sold</u> nine hundred?	No, we <u>bought</u> nine hundred.	Is that <u>I</u> as in <u>I</u>taly?
No, <u>A</u> as in <u>A</u>ustria.	Is that <u>thirty</u>?	No, <u>fifty</u>.	Is the <u>presentation</u> at three?	No, the <u>seminar</u> is at three.	So, <u>we</u> sold nine hundred?
No, <u>they</u> sold nine hundred.	Is that <u>A</u> as in <u>A</u>ustria?	No, <u>E</u> as in <u>E</u>gypt.	Is that <u>fifty</u>?	No, fif<u>teen</u>.	Is the <u>seminar</u> at three?

Instructions

1. Play with two to four people.
2. Each player takes seven dominoes.
3. Place one of the remaining dominoes in the middle and leave the others face down in a pile.
4. The first player places another domino at either end of the first one. This domino must have the question or response which matches the one on the end of the first domino. The player reads out the question and response, emphasising the stressed word or syllable.
5. The second player does the same and then the next player.
6. A player who can't go can pick one new domino from the pile and try to play.
7. The winner is the person who uses all his or her dominoes first or has the fewest at the end

Write your own 10 tips

Do you have 10 more ideas for Business English teachers?
Then why not write them down and share them with your colleagues?

1. ....
....
....
....
....

2. ....
....
....
....
....

3. ....
....
....
....
....

4. ....
....
....
....
....

5. ....
....
....
....
....

6.

....

....

....

....

....

7.

....

....

....

....

....

8.

....

....

....

....

....

9.

....

....

....

....

....

10.

....

....

....

....

....

ETpedia: 500 ideas for Business English teachers © Pavilion Publishing and Media Ltd and its licensors 2016.